The Good Mommies' Guide

to Raising

(Almost) Perfect Daughters

100 Tips on Raising Daughters Everyone Can't Help But Love

by Nonnie Jules

Nonnie Jules, Author
Email: nonniewrites@yahoo.com
Blog: http://nonniewrites.wordpress.com
Twitter: @nonniejules
Facebook: Nonnie Jules
Author Page: http://amazon.com/author/nonniejules

To the two most precious Daughters in all the world.
Thank you for your patience, not only throughout the writing of
this book, but for putting up with me for loving you too much, if
that is at all possible. You were truly my inspiration for every
word on every page. I did this in honor of you, so that you may
one day live in a world filled with more angelic, (Almost) Perfect
Daughters just like you.

To the Best Dad in all the world.
If not for you, there would be no (Almost) Perfect Daughters for
me to write about. Thank you for the role you have always
played, not just in the lives of our own daughters, but in the
lives of the many daughters who call you "Dad."

Table of Contents

The Good Mommy on...

Table of Contents (continued)

"THE GOOD MOMMIES' GUIDE TO RAISING (ALMOST) PERFECT DAUGHTERS"

100 Tips On Raising Daughters Everyone Can't Help But Love!

INTRODUCTION

The Bible (Proverbs 22:6) says: "Train up a child in the way he should go; even when he is old he will not depart from it." In honor of full disclosure, I must begin by saying that I AM NOT a doctor of any kind, I have no degree in child psychology and by no means at all am I perfect. What I am though, is the mother of an adult daughter and a teenage daughter. These Angel Daughters, as I call them, are truly (ALMOST) Perfect! They're honest, intelligent, driven, compassionate, loving, God-filled and very, very respectful.....all rolled up together. I often wonder how I was so blessed to be chosen as the one to mother them. My eldest daughter graduated high school, college and Grad school with her VIRGINITY still intact! How many moms can boast of that? And no matter how others may deny that keeping your virginity that long is no big deal, I know that it's something to really be proud of, especially since it's not the easiest thing to do. Not taking anything away from my husband, their father, because he has certainly been there every step of the way in guiding them, but because I did my part as a GOOD MOMMY to these two, I happily proclaim that I am a SPECIALIST in the child rearing department of Daughters.

My teenager, when asked why she will not consider becoming an attorney (because I think she'd make a really great one), responds with, "There is no way I could defend someone who might be guilty. I just couldn't do it, Mommy." I always tease her about becoming an attorney, just so I can hear this response. I never tire of it. Her character shines thru in that one little statement.

1

So many times, when our daughters take the wrong path, we wonder….. "What is wrong with HER? What is SHE doing wrong?" We fail to look inside at our own parenting skills where sometimes, the majority of the blame just might lie. Have you ever stopped to think *"What did I do wrong?"* *"What could I have done better?"* and going a step further *"Where did I fail her?"* So many Moms are busy focusing on themselves these days, when what they should really be focused on, are their kids...especially their daughters. I was blessed enough to be a stay-at-home mom for both of my Angel Daughters. They never had to go to daycare, they were never latch-key kids, and I was always, always there for them. But even if I had not been there, even if I had no choice but to go out and become a part of the workforce, I would have still made them my **top priority**. It is my deepest belief that if we spend more time nurturing, focusing and guiding our children, and less time trying to amass material things which will never be a direct reflection of us as parents, we would have more daughters who are ("Almost") perfect.

Speaking of (Almost) perfect Daughters, I recently picked up a copy of the much-talked-about book, **"Battle Hymn of the Tiger Mother,"** and I have to admit that I was in total agreement with her on some things, but then she lost me on some others. When she started comparing "Western" parents to Chinese mothers, of course suggesting the Chinese mothers were more superior in the parenting department, I instantly took a little offense. Now, in her book, Amy Chua (the Tiger Mother) says that there were things her two daughters were never allowed to do. Why they were never allowed to do these things I probably will never know, because I chose not to continue reading the book. *Not because of her parenting methods*, but because I continually felt as if I was being insulted by her comparisons of Chinese mothers and as she put it, her "Western Counterparts."

With that being said, here are some things she points out that her daughters were never allowed to do:
*Attend sleepovers *Have play dates *Be in school plays *Complain about not being in school plays *Watch TV or play computer games *Choose their own extracurricular activities *Get any grade less than an A *Not be the #1 student in every subject except PE and drama *Play any instrument other than the piano or violin *Not play the piano or violin.

The Tiger Mother went on to share her feelings on a few other things:
*Chinese immigrant mothers believe that their children can be the "best" students; that academic achievement reflects successful parenting, and that if children did not excel at school then there was a problem and parents were not doing their jobs; *Schoolwork always comes first; *an A- is a bad grade; *your children must be two years ahead of their classmates in math; *you must never compliment your children in public; *if your child ever disagrees with a teacher or coach, you must always take the side of the teacher or coach; *the only activities your children should be permitted to do are those in which they can eventually win a medal and *that medal MUST be gold.*

Now in contrast, here are some areas that she and I differ as well as where we are a bit similar:
*I believe that my daughters were the "best" students; that academic achievement does reflect successful parenting, and that if children are not excelling in school, parents are not doing **enough**; schoolwork ALWAYS comes first; there was a one "B" limit in our home and everything else had to be "A"s; children SHOULD be complimented whenever and wherever they deserve the compliment;*

not one teacher ever had a problem with either of my daughters, but I do remember I had problems with some teachers and would always begin my conversation with those teachers like this... "Now, if what you say doesn't mesh with what she has said, SHE will not be the one in trouble", (and when you know your kids the way I know mine, this is the ONLY way you should begin that type of conversation); my daughters were allowed to participate in any activity they so desired and lastly, they didn't have to win any type of award doing it.

Finally, I'd like to share direct quotes from the Tiger Mother: *"As I watched American parents slather praise on their children for the lowest of tasks – drawing a squiggle or waving a stick – I came to see that Chinese parents have two things over their Western counterparts: 1) higher dreams for their children and 2) higher regard for their children in the sense of knowing how much they can take." She went on to say that she did not want her children involved in just any activity, like crafts, "which can lead to nowhere," or even worse, playing the drums, "which leads to drugs," but rather a hobby that was meaningful and highly difficult with the potential for depth and virtuosity. And that's where the piano came in.*

I can understand why this Tiger Mother received such a backlash of disapproval when her book was released. Some called her a "tyrant", and while I was discussing her book in the book store with another Chinese mother, she referred to her as "way too extreme." I don't believe that we, as her Western Counterparts want any less for our Daughters. I believe that "Good" mothers around the world pray for the success and only want the very best for their children. We're all the same in that regard.

4

And I personally know some very successful people who have played the drums and were never on drugs, and I know of some who have turned their hobbies of crafting into very successful and lucrative businesses.

Now, although my daughters *HAVE participated in tons of sleepovers (with all of them being at our house), *watched tons of television, *played computer and video games, *played a musical instrument, *could not get any grade less than a "B", *had play dates, *were in school plays, they both turned out exceptionally well!

I had but one reason for sharing this mother's style of parenting, and that was to show that it is OK to have differences of opinions on parenting styles (without making the other party feel insulted, that is). What makes our world truly great is that we all don't have to agree on everything. Throughout *"*The Good Mommies' Guide* ...," YOU will not necessarily agree with some of my methods, but I ask that you please just appreciate and respect that they are MY methods, and they have worked very successfully for my Daughters. I truly believe that if you apply these tips to your own parenting, they can work just as well for yours. The Tiger Mother received a lot of backlash for her ideals on parenting, but just as I don't necessarily agree with ALL of her methods, I have to respect that they are HERS, and obviously she feels they worked for her daughters. I must say though that I do admire mothers who go that extra mile to ensure that their children are THE BEST as well as being AT THEIR BEST at all times. There is definitely nothing wrong with wanting your daughters to be successful in life and setting rules that must be followed, and imparting discipline at times is definitely not a bad route for you to take to get them there. For that, TIGER MOTHER, I applaud you.

This guide book was born out of the many questions I receive when someone meets my Daughters. I hear things like... *"They are so respectful and sweet. How did you get them to be that way?"* Although I am highly complimented when I'm asked these questions, they tend to amuse me immensely. But, my response is always the same, "It really wasn't that hard. I was just always very committed and consistent with my teachings."

Throughout this book you will find a few Bible scriptures here and there. This, in no way means that I will be "preaching" to you about anything, because I am definitely not the one equipped to do so. I live in a glass house so therefore, I will not be throwing any stones your way. *(Bible scripture clearly places the task of educating children not into the hands of some institution, but into the hands of the parents. They are called to "raise their children properly, so that they may not be a burden or even an evil to the community when they come of age").* The scriptures I have used throughout are here because first and foremost, my Daughters were raised in a Christian home, and they still are being raised in this manner. THAT is really the basis of their foundation. And although they come from a very loving household, their Parents couldn't be any more different. My husband Pastors in his church, I am a believer. My husband is in church faithfully, I rarely attend any services at all. His faith is extremely strong in God, and I am still trying to get there. I share all of this because I don't want you to be misled into thinking that we are these extreme parents and that is why our Daughters turned out as wonderfully as they did. So in answer to some of your "thoughts," NO, they were not SCARED STRAIGHT, it was the absolute opposite....they were loved all the way through and I'm just being honest about who we are. I want you to understand that you don't have to be a perfect Parent to raise (almost) perfect daughters. If that was a requisite for it, I would have never measured up.

6

To the new Mommys-to-be and to the Mommys with little ones still to be raised, please use this guide in your daily parenting and you will soon notice just how effective these tips really are. You will benefit the most from this guide because your daughters are still in your tummy OR they are newborns and toddlers, just starting out. The advantage that you have is you get to START EARLY!

To all the Dads out there who are serving as Mommys, too, you will especially benefit from some of these tips. Although your daughters may never run home to snuggle to watch a Lifetime movie with you, they will surely need you to show them how a lady is to be treated, how to change a flat tire and a host of other things that only a Dad/Mom can teach. And when you get to some of those tips that only a lady can teach a girl, that's when you enlist the help of those other very important people in your life. Your mom, sister, aunt or close friend will all do just fine.

Lastly, to all the mothers who feel, and to the ones who know for sure that they missed the boat in the proper rearing of their daughters, this book is especially for you. It is my wish for you, that should you become a new grandmother, godmother, adopted mother or guardian that you will use this guide as your second chance "do-over," which not many of us get in a lifetime. Take this opportunity to get it right, by raising that next generation the way they should be raised.

For those of you who like to read books with never-ending statistics and data, you won't find that here in *"The Good Mommies' Guide…"* Nope…not one detailed stat. I didn't have to go very far for research, as I lived this guide, day in and day out. What you will find though, are all the most important ways that I raised my daughters, my 100 TOP tips, filled with a lot of seriousness and a little humor thrown into the mix.

You will read real-life examples of certain situations as well as methods on how to deal with them. As I've mentioned before, I am far from being a perfect Mommy (just ask my Daughters), but I am a very good one, and while writing this book, I realized that there were some areas that I could have worked a little harder. So, just as you will learn from these tips, I have had to re-learn some as well. Hopefully, one day if and when GOD has blessed me with grand-daughters, that will be my chance to PERFECT on some of my very own tips. That will be MY do-over.

I'm going to end on this note... notice that the title of this book is not "THE "GREATEST" MOMMIES' GUIDE TO RAISING (ALMOST) PERFECT DAUGHTERS" it is very simply, *"The Good Mommies' Guide...."* Just as our daughters can be (almost) perfect, we should cut ourselves a little slack and accept that we don't have to be viewed as the GREATEST Mommys all the time. As long as we are caring, loving and giving our daughters the time and attention they need to become people that everyone can't help but love, the title of "GOOD" Mommy will always serve us just fine.

So get ready for the ride of your life as I share with you 100 of my TOP TIPS on how you, too can raise (ALMOST) PERFECT DAUGHTERS! Now this style of parenting may be a little too hard for some of you, like the parts where you have to consistently teach and teach and teach, but to others, you will smile, laugh and appreciate every single word. So hold on tight, because some of this ride might be a little too bumpy for you. But as in everything you do... Enjoy!

Nonnie Jules, Author
April, 2013

8

The Good Mommy on...

ABSTINENCE

1) **TEACH THEM THE IMPORTANCE OF ABSTINENCE UNTIL MARRIAGE.**
The Bible (1 Thessalonians 4:3-4) says "For this is the will of GOD, your sanctification; that you abstain from sexual immortality; that each of you know how to control her own body in holiness and honor". Today's society reeks of SEX, SEX, and more SEX everywhere we turn. Daughters are openly promiscuous, wild, foot loose and fancy free. Having the most sexual partners seems to be a competition to some. That is a sad state of affairs. People often ask me how did we get our daughter to hold on to her VIRGINITY as long as she has. I have said repeatedly, IT WAS NOT HARD AT ALL. It all goes back to starting to teach from the very beginning and also modeling the behavior you want to see in your daughter. I, by no means, kept my virginity as long as my Angel Daughter has kept hers, but she had been taught continually what the Bible had to say about it...and that summed up was simply "no sex outside of, and until marriage."

2) **EVEN IF SHE'S MADE THE DECISION TO DELAY SEX, YOU STILL NEED TO KEEP TALKING TO HER ABOUT IT.**
It is truly a blessing to hear your daughter say that she intends to keep her virginity until she is married...that she feels she is so special, she wants to save her virtue for that very special ONE person. But, although she has made that decision, this is one ball that you cannot just drop. I continually ask my daughter "So, do we need to have THE talk NOW?" I want to keep it in the forefront of her mind that this is a very important decision she has made and I want to continually remind her that if she is having any doubts, concerns, feelings or new questions that I'm here for her to always talk to.

9

ACCEPTANCE

3) INTRODUCE AND EDUCATE HER ON OTHER ETHNICITIES.

Just as a crayon box is filled with many different colors, so is the world in which we live. *Don't be afraid to introduce your daughter to other ethnicities and cultures. As a matter of fact, I will go so far as to say that THIS IS A MUST! If you want her to thrive in this world, expose her to more than just what is in her own backyard. Educate her so that she will know and understand that although we come in many different shades and skin tones, we all bleed one color and that is red. Teach her that people are just people, no matter the color of their skin. There truly is just one race and that's THE HUMAN ONE*!

4) TEACH HER TO APPRECIATE THE DIFFERENCES IN OTHERS.

No two people are alike and no two people were born exactly the same, not even twins. We live in a world of varied races and other orientations; therefore we must teach our daughters that it is OK to be different. Imagine how it would be to sit in a room where everyone looked like you, spoke like you, walked like you, dressed like you and had every thought the same as you. How boring would that be? Well, it would drive me absolutely MAD! It does my heart good to see children of all races and cultures, blue hair, red hair, brown eyes, grey eyes, hippie clothes, preppy clothes, just loving one another. *Teaching our daughters to appreciate the differences in others, is also teaching them acceptance and tolerance*, two things that it took us as a society a long time to overcome (on some levels) and two things that we are still struggling with today.

5)   **LOVE AND ACCEPT HER AS SHE IS**.
I personally have been very guilty of this one. I am this out-going, boisterous soul (and at times, a tad-bit too loud as my dear Granny puts it), and neither of my daughters are like me in this regard. In fact, they are the total opposite. They are their Dad's daughters. I remember early on getting very upset when my oldest daughter would not handle certain situations as I would have. I didn't feel as if she was really standing up for herself MY WAY. Then someone shared with me that she handles situations **in her own way**, and that should not upset me. She is her own person, right? I have since learned (and accepted) that although she doesn't deal with situations the way I would have her to, her way works just fine for her and is just as effective. We should love and accept our daughters just as they are. This was hard for me, but I did it.

6)   **LET HER HAVE SOME CONTROL OVER THE CAR RADIO. EVEN IF YOU DON'T LIKE HER MUSIC, PRETEND.**
Now this is a battle you just can't win. With having two daughters, one having been a teenager and the other in her teenage years now, I have had to give up control of the car radio (or either ride across town in total silence, because they were giving me the "treatment" for not sharing). _We don't have to like their music (they don't like ours, but they have to listen to it when riding in OUR cars), but at least pretend to. This shows that you really care about her and the things that interest her most_. And when you're really good at pretending, this will make her think you're a cool mom and then she will willingly show up to discuss things of other natures that might be going on with her. In the meantime, keep thinking that soon she'll have her own car and one day you'll be able to jump in and change the radio station to your kind of music! When she objects (and she will), just remind her… "But remember when…." Enough said.

The Good Mommy on...

BEING A LADY

7)   **TEACH HER HOW TO BE A LADY**.
Now this is truly my territory. I am definitely a Lady! Notice how I used the word "Lady" in reference to myself? That's because I detest being called a woman and I want to pull my hair out when I hear a man say "Hey Woman!", even jokingly. Have you ever heard anyone refer to the Queen of England as "That woman?" I think not! (Now throughout this guide you will notice that I do use the word **woman** quite a bit. That is because I have spoken with tons of females who find the use of this word, not offensive at all). I believe in walking around proudly with my head held high. I believe in proper etiquette in public, and out. I believe that chivalry is still alive. I believe that a man should always open doors for a lady, pull out her chair and even cover that big puddle of water with his jacket so she doesn't mess her shoes while crossing the street. It's lovely being a Lady isn't it? So, Ladies (Moms) lets teach and encourage our daughters to always remember these things and accept nothing less. Let us prepare them to do the work.

8)   **TEACH THEM MANNERS.**
Did you know that the Bible even speaks of manners? *(Proverbs 20:11) says "Even by his manners the child betrays whether his conduct is innocent and right*." We live in a manner-less society so when I see and hear young people, especially little children being manner-able, I stand in awe of the parents.

Teach your children at an early age to ALWAYS say Thank You, Please, Excuse me and most importantly...Yes Ma'am, No Ma'am, Yes Sir and No Sir. These little words will take them very far in life, I promise you. It's also nice to have table manners, too so how about enrolling your little darling in an upcoming etiquette class?

The Good Mommy on...

BOYS & MEN

9)   **TEACH THEM HOW TO SET LIMITS WITH BOYS**.
'Boys will be boys', as the saying goes, but what does that really mean? Well, to me it means that they will do what they are allowed to do...in their homes, with their parents, in school and yes, with the girls. We have to teach our daughters that they should never put themselves in any kind of compromising position with the opposite sex. We have to teach them to say NO and to mean NO any time they find themselves in situations that are too mature for their liking.   Boys distract and sometimes cause our daughters to defer their futures. We must instill in them that they have plenty of time to incorporate boys into their lives, but only **after** they have achieved their goals, realized their dreams and have established themselves, independent   of   anyone   else.

10)   **TEACH HER HOW TO EXPECT TO BE TREATED BY A MAN. THEN SHE'LL KNOW WHEN SHE'S NOT BEING TREATED WELL AND WILL REFUSE TO TOLERATE IT**.
This is really a touchy subject for me. Maybe because I've been around so many women who have been mistreated or abused by men. I think GOD allowed me to witness those situations so that I could somehow counsel and encourage those women to think more of themselves and get away from their abusers. I have long stressed that a man will do whatever a woman allows him to. That being said, when you have daughters and they see and hear men disrespecting and mistreating you, what kind of message do you think you're sending to them? What do you think you're teaching them by showing them this?" Well, let me answer this question for you: when daughters see their mothers being disrespected, whether verbally, physically,

emotionally, or mentally, the daughters learn that this behavior is acceptable. This saddens me because these very daughters will grow up and repeat this cycle. They, in turn will think that it is OK for men to abuse them by those same methods.

I consider myself a very strong lady, and NO MAN has ever been allowed, nor will one ever be allowed to do anything but treat me like the Queen that I am, and so that is the message, and the ONLY message that I have sent my daughters in regards to how they should be treated by the opposite sex. They have also had many years of seeing first-hand how a man should treat a Lady because I put a perfect example in front of them...their Father. So, if you don't want to ever knock on your daughter's door and see her sporting a new black eye, then how about not ever walking around in front of her wearing a patch or cover to hide the one some man gave you. If you want to see this strength in your daughters, then you have to model it for them. Show them how strong you are and how much you love and value yourself by not accepting mistreatment or abuse from anyone. You can't say to her "It is not OK for a man to speak to you that way," when all she has ever heard were verbal assaults flung at you. I spoke with an outreach counselor in regards to this particular tip because I wanted to be sensitive to women who have found themselves in situations such as these. I did learn some things that I can readily admit to being ignorant about, but I will simply say this... ***The FIRST time a man hits you, you don't stick around for a second. Teach your daughter that if a man can't respect her, then it's time for him to move on***.

11)   TEACH HER THAT NO MAN IS WORTH BETRAYING ANOTHER WOMAN FOR.

Women today just don't have enough respect for one another, but the ultimate disrespect is when a woman gets involved with another woman's boyfriend or husband. There are enough men in this world that it is so unnecessary to get involved with one who's already otherwise engaged. _Teach your daughter to never, ever disrespect another woman by betraying her with her boyfriend or husband. Then go a step further and teach her to have more respect for herself than to stoop to this lowest of levels_. She must always keep in the forefront of her brain, that no man is worth betraying another woman. Even if you don't know that other woman.

BULLYING

12)   TEACH HER THAT BULLYING IS A SERIOUS ISSUE.
Would you like my opinion of bullying? Well, here it is: I think it should be labeled a very serious crime. I also think that the culprits should be punished to the highest extent of the law, no matter their ages! We, as parents have the responsibility of teaching our children how they are to treat other people. And sadly, some bullies learn to bully from their very own parents. *Teach your daughter that bullying is a crime, and that it is never OK to join in when there is a group bullying session taking place. Teach her to report instances where she feels most uncomfortable about what's being done to someone else and most importantly, make her feel comfortable in coming to you sharing any and everything that might be happening to her that makes her uncomfortable or afraid.* Children are literally being bullied to death and it's time that parents step in and take responsibility of knowing their children, at home AND away from home.

13)   TEACH HER TO STAND UP FOR HERSELF AND OTHERS.
Ironically, the previous tip was about bullying and here we are teaching our daughter to stand up for herself and others. *There are times when you should just walk away from situations and then there are those times when you just need to stand your ground to let the offending party know that you are not the one. Not the one to be picked on. Not the one to be harassed. Not the one to be pushed around.* Now, I am in no way condoning violence of any kind and standing your ground and standing up for yourself does not mean that you have to resort to or engage in anything physical. It simply means SPEAKING to the offender asking them to back off, because you will not stand for anything

else. Sometimes you just have to look a bully in the eye and let him/her know that you mean business. Furthermore, it is A-O-K to come to the defense of someone who you see is being bullied or mistreated. I do it all the time. My husband says I am a rebel with many causes. Whatever that means, I just have zero tolerance for people mistreating other people and something inside me compels me to come to the defense of others I see being bullied or mistreated. Sometimes you just have to stand up for others. When you see that they are not strong enough to do it for themselves, you STAND in their stead and know that you are doing an awesome thing, You Hero!

COMPLIMENTS

14)   TEACH HER TO ACCEPT COMPLIMENTS GRACEFULLY.
Have you ever noticed that when someone gives you a compliment, especially when you feel you're not looking your best, you make excuses for your appearance **before** you even say *'thank you'*? I am guilty of this a lot. This is just madness, though. _We should teach our daughters that beauty is definitely in the eyes of the beholder, and although WE DON'T THINK that we are looking our best at that moment, someone else may be thinking we look like a million dollars. We can't see what the other person is seeing so just say THANK YOU with a smile, and move on_.

15)   ENCOURAGE HER TO COMPLIMENT OTHER LADIES WITH SINCERITY.
"A candle loses nothing by lighting another candle." This sign hangs on the wall of my office, reminding me daily that "I am merely a candle burning bright and I am eager and willing to light your fire, so that you, too can burn and shine ever so brightly, just like me. And after having lit your fire, I have lost nothing. I am still on fire, still burning and shining brightly as ever!" Every time I walk out of my door, no matter where I am, if there is another woman in sight, I find something about her to compliment. Whether it's her hair, her eyes, her shoes, her clothes, or even the beautiful smile that's splashed across her face, I acknowledge it.   So many times, women walk around, eyeing each other, envious of this person they know nothing about, wishing them no good at all. What they should be doing instead is looking at this Lady as if they were looking in the mirror at themselves, loving the person they see, only wanting to lift her up.

The Bible (1 Thessalonians 5:11) says "Therefore encourage one another and build one another up…" That's what SHOULD be done…we should spend more time lifting each other up instead of trying to tear one another down. *Teach your daughter to find SOMETHING good in EVERY woman she sees, and to compliment that woman for that beautiful thing, no matter what it is, no matter how small.* With all of us teaching our daughters to love and respect other women, then there will be very little room for the green-eyed monster to rear her ugly head.

16) **COMPLIMENT ALL HER GOOD QUALITIES, NOT JUST HER LOOKS**.

When we hold them in our arms for the very first time, all we see is their beauty. We are amazed later in life to find that they have morphed into so much more than that beauty. They are intelligent, kind, caring, loving and God-fearing little creatures. We should *consistently compliment all of these so that they will know that what makes them so special is more than that gorgeous face GOD gave them*.

17) **REINFORCE HOW WONDERFUL AND WORTHY SHE IS**.

Now I will readily admit that I am what most would call AN EXTREME MOM (in a good way). Unlike some though, I don't see that as a negative thing at all. Actually, it's a testament to why my daughters turned out the way they did. I mean, I truly do love and adore my daughters to the extreme. Every day of their lives, I would take pictures of them, to the point that when they saw me pointing my phone or camera in their direction, they would either run, duck or turn away. My daughter lived 5 hours away at college and had to send me a picture of her, every day. She tired of this, but I missed her so much, I just asked her to humor her old, loving Mommy!

And just like a Mommy who has to work and miss every "first" in her toddler's life, with my baby being so far away, I didn't want to miss anything she was doing. I wanted to see her pretty face every day, just as if she was still at home. But, for the most part, I think they're used to it by now (because I still do it). They still don't like it, but I still do it. Every single day I tell them how much I love and adore them and just how wonderful and special they are. Here is an actual text conversation between myself and my oldest daughter just recently: <**Mommy**> *"U are the most exceptional 20 something year old daughter in the whole world. I am always in such awe of you! I admire u so much and am so very proud to be Ur mother!"* <**Daughter**> *"Thank you, Mommy for CONSTANTLY reminding me of how proud u r...keeps me pushin'. Love you, goodnight!"*

And here is another text conversation between me and my teenage daughter: <**Mommy**> *"Mommy loves u sooooo much! Don't ever doubt that. Do you know it?"* <**Daughter**> *"Yes, ma'am, I do!"* If we uplift, show and tell our daughters how special and how loved they are on a consistently regular basis, they will have no need to go outside seeking that kind of attention or love from any boy or a man. Give them what they need inside, so that the wrong person doesn't come along and do it for you.

DISCIPLINE

18)   DON'T BE AFRAID TO DISCIPLINE WHEN IT'S NEEDED.

Again, in full disclosure I must say that I have never physically disciplined my daughters, BUT, that was only because I didn't have to. I had 4 siblings and I come from the school where whippings were just a part of life, and I also tend to think, we all turned out pretty well. I believe that some children only need verbal chastisement, but then others....well, that's when we need to invoke the teachings of the Bible. **(Proverbs 22:15) says: "Folly is bound up in the heart of a child, but the rod of discipline will drive it far from him."** I know that people differ on this subject; some believe in physical discipline, others believe in only verbal, and some don't believe in it at all...and that's OK (as long as they keep them at their house). I personally believe that parents should be allowed to discipline their children in the way THEY SEE FIT for their family. That being said, a child should never be bruised, injured or cut by a physical correction. *The Bible (Ephesians 6:4 & Colossians 3:21) warns that parents should not abuse the power and authority they have over their children while they are young because it provokes the children to "righteous anger."* Physical discipline should always be done in love and never as a vent to the parent's frustration. It is also just one part of discipline and should ONLY be used when the child shows defiance to a clear limit, not in the heat of the moment. No matter how it's done, don't be afraid to do it. *I must end this by re-iterating that discipline is something that you need to begin at an early age, and when I say early age, I mean day ONE*! You cannot wait until your child is 13, 14 or even 16 years old, standing taller than you, and decide that they're a little too-mouthy for you. If you start from day one, I can assure you, "mouthing off" will never be a problem.

DRUGS & ALCOHOL

19) TEACH YOUR DAUGHTERS ABOUT THE CONSEQUENCES OF DRUG USAGE.

Schools are now taking responsibility for teaching kids about drugs and their harmful effects. We are the parents, so it is first and foremost our responsibility to do this. Inform your daughter that those who abuse drugs of any kind (alcohol included) can die at a very early age, go to jail and also have a very hard life, all because they decided to use drugs. _Let them know that drug usage at school, at a party or even among friends can turn into an addiction that has the potential to ruin their lives_.

20) TEACH HER NEVER TO GET INTO A CAR WITH SOMEONE WHO HAS BEEN DRINKING.

Drinking alcohol to me is just as bad as doing drugs. Either way, when under the influence you can hurt yourself or even worse, you can hurt someone else. _Teach your daughter that it is NEVER OK, under any circumstances to get in a car with someone who is under the influence of ANY drug, alcohol included._ Did I stress NEVER? Let her know that no matter where she is, no matter how far away, all she has to do is pick up the phone and call you to come and pick her up, no questions asked. Then let her know how proud you are that she made such a smart decision on her own.

EDUCATION

21)   POST SPELLING WORDS ON THE FRIDGE.

I love words. Just as I love books, I truly love words. I like to sit and just read the dictionary sometimes. When both my daughters were very young, I introduced them to Ms. Merriam. You know Merriam don't you? Merriam Webster? Well, she's a dictionary and she knows EVERYTHING. She holds the key to unlock the spelling, the definition and the pronunciation of WONDERFUL WORDS. Words open the windows to our children's minds and imaginations. They introduce them to worlds far beyond their reach, and they can take them places they never thought they'd go. It is impressive to have an extensive vocabulary, and I think it a shame to limit your ability to communicate simply because your vocabulary is limited to a very few and very simple words. Encourage your daughters to fall in love with the dictionary. I did, simply by hanging weekly NEW, college-aged words behind a magnet on my fridge door. And weekly, they learned the spelling, the definition, the pronunciation AND they had to use each in a sentence, while, incorporating these new words into their everyday conversations. Talk about impressive! When my teenager was in kindergarten, my oldest daughter was in junior high and each day when we got out of the car to go inside to collect her after school, the Principal, who knew of my daughters' extensive vocabulary, would always say to her "What's the word bird?" And as she spewed off a few of her "new" words, he would scramble to find his dictionary. Seriously, these were words a school PRINCIPAL didn't even know. *Don't be afraid to challenge their minds. They will always come out on top because you always kept them ahead.*

22)   **MAKE EDUCATION A HIGH PRIORITY**.

Academics have always been, and always will be priority in OUR home. My youngest daughter is a big sports girl, and my oldest has super-stardom on the brain. And although it's wonderful that they're involved in outside activities and have very high aspirations, they have always known that school was their most important job. Parents need to step away from the mentality of "SPORTS BEING THE END ALL" for their kids. It's great to want to be the top quarterback in the NFL, but what happens if you get a busted knee and are out for the rest of the season, or even worse, you get a head injury and can never play sports again? Then you need to have a Plan B...and for most, that's what education is. Education in my home is and always has been Plan A, and everything else is just an add-on. *Teach your kids that although you can fail at a sport, you can never fail by getting an education*.

23)   **DON'T WAIT FOR HER GRADES TO SLIP BEFORE YOU BECOME INVOLVED. BE INVOLVED FROM DAY ONE.**

Every year that my daughters were in school, my husband and I regularly visited their campuses. As a very active member of the parent organization on my child's campus, I tried to get more parents involved in their children's educations; sometimes I was successful, other times, not so much. It's really sad to see that the only times you see parents at school is when their kids come home with a bad grade. What's so hard about showing up before then? Taking the time, to spend some time letting your daughter know that you are very interested in her education and that it is top priority, is the sign of a really GOOD parent. Don't wait for a bad grade to come home. Encourage and help her so that she understands if she is struggling, you are there to help. *Be involved from day one and your daughter will probably never have a bad grade day to begin with*.

24)   **SET HIGH EDUCATIONAL EXPECTATIONS FOR HER.**
Isn't it a wonderful feeling to graduate high school? But, what about the feeling after four years of college? Well, if you loved those feelings, can you imagine the high you'd be on after having received your Masters or PhD? Some parents are just happy their kids made it out of high school and could really care less if they ever went through college. They see high school as a very high achievement.   Not in our family.   Although my husband and I both attended college because we wanted to, college and grad school were not options for our daughters. Going to college in our home was a given. Just as you knew you had to go to elementary school, you KNEW you would have to attend college. *Encourage your daughter to always go further than what is generally expected of her. If your educational expectations for your daughters are set high, then reaching for the stars and landing on the moon is what they'll give you*.

25)   **HELP HER TO DEVELOP TRAITS THAT ARE CONSIDERED PRIMARILY MASCULINE TRAITS – SUCH AS PROFICIENCY IN MATH AND SCIENCE. THESE WILL HELP HER LATER IN LIFE.** I was not a Math or Science person when I was in school. I'm still not a math and science person, but I really wished I could have been. I looked upon people who excelled in, and who loved these subjects as total geniuses. In my mind, if you were a math and/or science wiz, you could rule the world. I now have a teenage Math & Science little genius of my own and I am in awe of her and how enthused she is for something that, to someone like me, appears to be so very difficult. She lights up when you say MATH. She totally beams if there is an experiment to be made. When you have daughters who shy away from these subjects, support and encourage them to not give up on excelling in these subjects which are considered "masculine" subjects.

I heard a female doctor say recently that when she was in college her first year, she failed Math. The feeling that she had from that failure, caused her to spend the rest of her time on that college campus almost living in the math lab. And she eventually GOT IT! She said if it had not been for her dad telling her that "she could do it," she would have given up after that first horrible grade. _Let's help our daughters to keep at it, until they get it._ And they are all so very smart, that I know eventually they will!

ENCOURAGEMENT

26) ENCOURAGE HER, WHETHER SHE WINS OR LOSES, SO THAT SHE UNDERSTANDS THE VALUE OF GOOD SPORTSMANSHIP.

Have you ever really watched a sore loser after a game loss? They have an ugly scowl on their face, they're angry and they storm off the court with the quickness of a flick of the middle finger. It is so sad to watch. Obviously, no one ever taught them the value of good sportsmanship. *The best thing you can do for your daughter, whether she's competing in a sport or a spelling bee, is to teach her that "it doesn't matter if you win or lose it's how you play the game." Encourage her in and out of victories, so that she will be capable of applauding and congratulating the winning team, even though she played on the losing one.*

27) BE A COACH WITH HER, NOT A JUDGE.

Coaches encourage, not criticize. They critique, they don't judge. Parents who are continuously judgmental alienate their children because the children feel like they are against them. *Anything your daughter is involved in, she's expecting encouragement from you, not judgment, so be careful not to confuse the two. Never forget, the greatest barrier to her success could be too much criticism from you (Mom), so take it easy.* Now who's been guilty of this? (My hand is raised extremely high!!!)

28) **DON'T TELL HER THAT HER PERFORMANCE WAS GOOD, WHEN IT TRULY WASN'T**.

This is where some parents fail and I'm sure this is where I will also be compared to the Tiger Mom. LISTEN TO ME CLOSELY.....How do you expect your child to improve her performance, if you continually tell her that her poorest performance was great? She will think, "Cool, I don't need to work harder, I'm already there." This is a big mistake a lot of parents make for the sake of what they call "trying not to belittle their child." This is not "belittling", this is called constructive criticism. _When you let your daughter know that her performance could have been better, you're only helping and encouraging her to work harder on improving it._

EXTRA-CURRICULAR STUFF

29) MAKE SURE SHE STAYS PRODUCTIVE, NOT IDLE AND WASTEFUL OF TIME.
It is amazing how so many kids get caught up in wasting time by procrastinating, but that's what they're supposed to do, right? They're kids! It is our job as parents to guide them down more productive avenues.   Video games, texting, InstaGram, Facebook and Twitter, just won't cut it. I strongly encourage you to limit the time they spend on these social networking sites. *Have a conversation with your daughter and find out what she's most interested in. If she says modeling, well, enroll her in modeling school. If she wants to play Basketball or Soccer, then find her a team*. There is more to life than what the internet offers our children, and the less time they spend there (unless it's for academic reasons), the better. Oh, and don't forget, no one was ever sorry for spending too much time in the library!

30) INVOLVE YOUR DAUGHTERS IN EXTRA-CURRICULAR ACTIVITIES.
Girls that are involved in activities such as sports, youth groups, girl clubs, etc. don't have time to engage in idleness of mind. They are too busy developing themselves and their skills for their futures. These girls, more often than not, become great leaders of our society as opposed to the daughters who are left to attend to their own devices, between only home and school. Activities don't have to be costly, either. *Take your daughters to museums, the theatre, live plays in the parks, afternoon teas with their friends and their moms where they're honing their social skills; anything positive that will keep them engaged and out of mischief*.

FAMILY

31) **TEACH THEM THE IMPORTANCE OF PUTTING FAMILY FIRST, AFTER GOD**.

My family eats together, we play together, we travel together and yes, we pray together. When we're invited places, the hosts can always expect to see the four of us. I jokingly say "we are a packaged deal." Since there are no other siblings, just my two daughters, I have instilled in them how important they are to one another and how… after Mommy and Daddy are gone from this earth, they will ONLY have each other. I have always taught my eldest daughter, that even when she marries, she should never put anyone before her sister. I tell them both that "If one of you strike it rich and become famous, so will your sister automatically become rich and famous. _Teach your daughters to always take care of each other and family first, after GOD!_ Although the famous Kardashian clan should not serve as good role models **on many levels** because of their very crude behaviors and foul mouths towards their mom, in one capacity, they have my vote. They are a very close-knit family, and it warms my heart to see them always caring for, and in defense and support of one another. The Braxton sisters would have my vote here as well. And all of them, Kardashians & Braxtons alike are just so cute together!

32) **SPEND QUALITY TIME WITH HER**.

Contrary to popular belief, Daughters love spending time with their Mothers, no matter the age or stage of their lives, but it's something you have to establish early on. You can't (or shall I say **you shouldn't**) just pop up one day when she's 16 and say "Hey, want to go to a movie?" She will think that you're going through some kind of mid-life crisis or worse, that you've been dumped by your friends or all the other things that you've spent your time on for the past 15 years of her life. My daughters and I spend quality time together on a very regular basis. We have movie dates, lunch dates, dinner dates, pamper dates...I seem to have more dates with my daughters than I do with my husband. These are special bonding times for us. We have girl talk and so much more love-filled moments during these times. So just remember, *it doesn't matter what you spend time doing, as long as you spend time doing it regularly together, and it would also be nice if you started sooner than later*.

33)   MAKE SURE SHE AND DAD SPEND LOTS OF TIME TOGETHER.

I didn't grow up with my dad so it was so very important to me that my daughters have a really great relationship with their dad. And do they ever! They do everything together, and a lot of times, those things don't include me (and that's fine....because they all like being outdoors and I don't do dirt, bugs and birds). Sometimes the three of them gang up on me in conversations or family meetings, and I love that, too! When they were younger, if he left their sight, they would cry until he returned. Me, not so much. This would probably make some Moms jealous, but I love that they have a very special bond, exclusive of me. He belongs to them and they definitely belong to him. When parents aren't together, especially in the same home, children tend to suffer, even if it's not noticeable immediately. A daughter needs her Father just as much as she needs her Mother, so encourage her to spend lots of time with her Dad. Never speak ill of her Father in her presence if the two of you don't have a really positive relationship. Always remember that she loves him, just as she loves you. Encourage this bond because he will ultimately be the one to show her how a man is to behave around a lady and how a man is to treat a lady. He should be her first teacher in this class.

34) **ENCOURAGE HER TO SPEND TIME WITH HER GRANDMOTHER. FOR SOME STRANGE REASON, THEY WILL GET ALONG FABULOUSLY.**

I know of many Mother/Daughter relationships that stay on rocky ground. I mean, no matter how the two try to make it work, they just can't get it together. This truly saddens me because I could not even bear the thought of not having a close relationship with either of my Angel Daughters. BUT, just because you may have one of these relationships with your own mother, does not mean that your daughter can't have a very positive, loving one with her. Don't have negative conversation with your daughter in regards to her grandmother nor should you ever speak ill of your mother in your daughters' presence. If the distance between the two of you has spilled over into her feelings of her grandma, sway those feelings in a positive direction. If she doesn't have a relationship with her grandma now, encourage her to pick up the phone to call her and also, encourage her to go and spend time with her. Maybe, just maybe, your beautiful daughter may have just been the missing piece that will connect you and your mom once again.

FORGIVENESS

35)   **TEACH YOUR DAUGHTER FORGIVENESS.**   *The Bible (Ephesians 4:32) says "Be kind to one another, tenderhearted, forgiving one another, as GOD in Christ forgave you."*
It's not always easy to forgive someone, especially when they have wronged or hurt you horribly, but the Bible teaches us to forgive less we be not forgiven. I have always shared with my daughters that when you've been hurt, let down or betrayed, it's OK to forgive. Forgiveness does not mean forgetting, as you can forgive a person without excusing the hurtful act.

FRIENDSHIP

36)   **TEACH THEM HOW IMPORTANT IT IS TO BE A GOOD, TRUST WORTHY FRIEND**.

The Bible (Proverbs 11:13) says "Whoever goes about slandering reveals secrets, but he who is trustworthy in spirit keeps a thing covered" and *The Bible (John 15:13) says "Greater love has no one than this: to lay down one's life for one's friends."*

Good friends are hard to come by and sometimes, if you have not been given the tools, it's even harder to BE a good friend to others. In the beginning, I taught my daughters to always share their toys. As they got older, I taught them the importance of being loyal and if someone confided a secret to them, to take that secret to the grave, unless someone was being hurt or abused.   They were taught that if someone had something negative to say about another person, to either dismiss the conversation by letting the offending party know they did not wish to engage in such conversation, or by removing themselves from the conversation altogether. My daughters are viewed as such great friends, that they are the ones that their friends come to for advice. They are the ones pegged as good listeners with the best shoulders to lean on and they are the "GO-TO" gals when you're looking for a good, trust-worthy friend. Equip your daughters early on with the proper tools so that they will know how to receive good friendships as well as know how to give of themselves in that same department.

37)   **TEACH YOUR DAUGHTERS TO BE GOOD LISTENERS**.
Sometimes, people just need a caring ear. They don't need you to say much, they just need you to listen. _Teach your daughters my 5-second rule: always wait 5 seconds after someone finishes speaking, before they open their mouth to say a word_. This ensures that the speaker has finished completely and is now opening the floor for any comments and/or concerns.

GOALS & DREAMS

38)   TEACH THEM THE IMPORTANCE OF GOAL-SETTING.
Everyone has to have a plan. To get to where you want to be, you have to map out how you will get there. I've always encouraged my daughters to set goals, to map out that blueprint for their lives. Commit your goals to paper and post that paper where you can see it every day. It will serve as a reminder of what you're working towards. When you set goals, you have dreams. And who wouldn't want to work hard to see their dreams realized?

39)   TEACH THEM THE IMPORTANCE OF REACHING GOALS AND FULFILLING DREAMS "BEFORE" LIFE SETS IN.
Now that goals have been set, it's time to reach them. Go after reaching these goals with gusto! It's imperative that we impart on our daughters the significance of reaching goals and fulfilling dreams BEFORE life sets in.   Boyfriends, Fiancés, Husbands, Babies, homes and mini vans won't be all that appealing until life has been lived to the fullest. (What, you're not excited about the minivan?)   And, when your daughters look around and see all that they have accomplished on their own, that's the time they will say, "OK, now I'm ready for a family of my own."
Remember, GOD created for six days and on the seventh he rested. *Encourage your daughters to create the lives they want for themselves FIRST by working hard*, then their family will be their reward and serve as their seventh day.

40)   **ENCOURAGE HER TO DEVELOP DREAMS AND TO FOCUS PRIMARILY ON THOSE THAT ARE ATTAINABLE.**

Here we go dreaming again, right?   Well, dreams are very important.   To dream is to allow your mind to travel to places you might not ever get to visit or to lay the ground work for what's to come in your life.   It's good to dream so do encourage your daughter to dream, and dream, and then dream some more.   Although it's OK to dream, we need to ensure that what's taking up space in her mind is something that's really attainable.   It's OK to want to grow up to be a Princess, but what is the likelihood of that unless you're a relative of the Queen of England?   Let's turn that dream around by encouraging her to want to become a King….like the PRESIDENT OF THE UNITED STATES OF AMERICA! (I know I said KING. We can be ANYTHING we want to be, remember?)

41)   **TEACH HER TO BE OPEN-MINDED ABOUT HER CAREER PATH, WHETHER IT'S TRADITIONAL OR NON-TRADITIONAL.**

As little girls playing in dollhouses, bandaging our little baby dolls from their imaginary wounds, maybe we dreamed of becoming a nurse.   As we moved on to Jr. High school, maybe we were so enamored with our favorite teacher   that we wanted to become one just like her.   And then there was high school, and somehow we had once again changed our minds and now wanted to become a dancer.   No matter the course your daughter chooses as her career path, teach her to always remain open-minded.   Where is it written that once you decide on one career, that you have to be stuck there?   It's not written anywhere.   Encourage her to consider all her options when it's time to make that choice, but should the wind start blowing her in another direction, then by all means, be gone with the wind, Fabulous!

GOD, FAITH & THE CHURCH

42)   TEACH THEM TO ALWAYS PUT GOD FIRST.
When we teach our daughters to put GOD first, it seems that everything else in their life just falls into place, in perfect order. If your daughter is grounded in faith, then she will learn how to better cope when she is faced with hardships and negative situations. Let her know that just as getting up and dressing for a Saturday night on the town is really important to her, then so, too is getting up the next morning being the first one in church. Give God his time and he will give you yours!

43)   TEACH THEM WHY FAITH AND CHURCH ARE IMPORTANT. *The Bible (Hebrew 10:25) says: "Let us not give up meeting together, as some are in the habit of doing, but let us encourage one another – and all the more as you see the Day approaching (NIV)."*
The Bible instructs us to be in relationship with other believers. If we are part of Christ's body, we will recognize our need to fit into the body of believers. When our daughters are young, very young….that is the time when we should take them to church and get them involved in the positive-ness of church. I say that because, let's be honest, there is a negative side to it as well (i.e. the gossip-mongers in the parking lot after Sunday service.
We don't want to be a party to this, now do we?)   If you start them off early, then they will learn and grow into their faith. They will make it a regular part of their lives and will in turn take, and teach their own children the importance of FAITH, their religion and why going to the church will feed their spirits and their souls. The church is the place where Christians come together to encourage one another as members of Christ's

body. My husband is a Pastor and our Daughters have always been raised in a Christian home. Although I personally do not have a church home at this time, my daughters have never wavered in their attendance and commitment to their faith and the church. The basis of whom and what they are, truly stems from their relationship with GOD.

GOSSIP

44)   **TEACH YOUR DAUGHTERS NOT TO GOSSIP.** *The Bible (Matthew 12:36-37) says: "I assure you, on judgment day people will be held accountable for every unguarded word they speak. By your words you will be acquitted, and by your words you will be condemned."* Now, this can be a hard one because the one thing I do believe is that females love to talk! And sometimes, that talking is not for the good of any. Beginning when my teenage daughter was in 1st grade, she would get in the car and we would have these girlfriend-like conversations. I would say "So tell me, what happened in school today?" And from there, she would spill the beans about everything and everybody. My husband would look on in horror and ask, "You do realize she's only six right?" I told him I was very aware of her age. The reason we had these conversations is because neither of my daughters were allowed to talk to anyone about anyone else, EVER! This is what I call "MESS" and mess was not allowed to stand on my porch, let alone knock at my door. There's one very positive lesson that I learned from my own mother. She would say… "Where you find mess, you leave it," and that's the way I have raised my daughters. If you realize that a person you call your friend is "messy", then by all means, just like on Facebook, "de-friend" her (is that what they call it?) My adult daughter, who is more like her dad than my teenage daughter, would never have a cross word to say about anyone anyway. She would pray for you before she ever gossiped about you, and she is still that way today. My teenage daughter though, is a little more like me.

She just has to get it out at times, and so she was only allowed (and still is only allowed) to get it out with me. Let's face it, we are only human, but in spite of that we *should teach our daughters not to gossip, and that going from one person to another having conversations about others, is just wrong*. I am an adult now and the one person that I spill the beans with about everything and EVERYBODY, is my 83 yr. old grandmother. Funny story here: my teenage daughter walked in the room one day while I was chatting over the phone with my dear Granny and after listening to my conversation for a minute, she shakes her head and says..."Mommy, it's time to get some new friends because you have hit rock bottom. You are on the phone GOSSIPPING with your grandmother." Well, darling, if that's my rock-bottom, I will take it any day. At least I will never have to worry about what I'm sharing with her getting back to anyone on the street! AND... my granny and I don't gossip. We share. *So, if your daughter just needs to vent and get her feelings out about something or someone she's not happy with, ENSURE that she gets it out with you AND ONLY YOU or her precious DEAR DIARY!*

GRATITUDE

45) **TEACH HER TO WRITE HAND WRITTEN THANK YOU NOTES. FOR EVERYTHING**.

Some of you might be thinking "hand written Thank You Notes? Isn't simply saying THANK YOU enough?" And my direct answer to that is…ABSOLUTELY NOT!   A THANK YOU note should be given for the smallest gesture, or even kind words uttered, that made a day brighter. A spoken "THANK YOU" is not remembered as long, or as well as a handwritten note. Teach your daughters to always keep blank THANK YOU notes on hand at all times (I always keep a pack in my car and an individual one in my purse, just in case I run into a THANK YOU that needs to be given immediately). You just never know when you will be in that moment when an on-the-spot THANK YOU might be warranted or needed.

46) **TEACH HER TO KEEP A GRATITUDE JOURNAL**.

The Bible (1 Thessalonians 5: 16-18) says: "Rejoice evermore. Pray without ceasing. In everything give thanks." My daughters were taught to pray when they were toddlers. Although they probably didn't understand what they were doing, it still got them in the habit of praying. As they got older, they learned to be grateful for EVERYTHING in their lives, the good and the bad. (My 20 something year old daughter thanks God before she even puts a piece of candy in her mouth! Thank you, Jesus!) As teenagers, they have always been encouraged to keep a gratitude journal. Each night before they lie down to sleep, they jot down 10 things that they are grateful for that day. I also keep a gratitude journal and on the days when my sun isn't shining, and my skies are just so dark and grey, I open my journal and it reminds me of all the things I have to be thankful for. _Teach your own daughter to find ten blessings a day and to write them down in her gratitude journal. Twenty on bad days_.

HER PERSONAL SELF

47)   TEACH HER ABOUT PUBERTY BEFORE IT HAPPENS.

My mom never talked to me or my sisters about a menstrual cycle. I remember learning about it in 6th grade when a fellow student of mine had a little accident while wearing her favorite white pants (I guess her mom didn't talk to her about it, either). Fast forward to my daughter being in 4th grade and the school is about to show the girls a film about puberty. At first, I was a little resistant to my 4th grader learning about the birds, the bees and also <periods>, but I was glad that she was getting this early lesson about the changes in her body in the comfort of her peers. In my eyes, she was definitely still my little baby, but they are growing up a little faster these days. The more I thought about it, the more it began to make sense to me. The film opened the door for the discussion and made it all that much easier (and more comfortable) for a lot of the moms to broach the subject with their daughters. After the film, the school supplied all the girls with their very own little personal pouches, which included a sanitary pad. After picking my daughter up from school that day, we went to the nearest pharmacy and I purchased her very own full pack of sanitary pads, and told her that she should always keep one in her purse "just in case." Now, my daughters are always prepared no matter when Mother Nature decides to drop by. _Don't be afraid to teach your daughter about puberty and introduce her to Mother Nature early, so she's never caught off guard should that wicked little lady happen to show up unexpectedly._

48)   **FOCUS ON BEING HEALTHY, NOT BEING SLIM**.
Almost every magazine you pick up today has pictures of pencil-thin models. Our daughters are bombarded with these images and made to think that this is the norm. IT IS NOT! Do your research so you will be able to intelligently explain to your daughter what these models do to stay so thin, and how it is the nature of that business to stay so thin. Let her know that the methods used, are clearly sometimes deadly. *Whether they are a size 4 or a size 14, we must stress to our daughters that they are loved regardless. Encourage them to focus on always being healthy, and less-focused on being thin*. Most health enthusiasts tend to believe that healthy and thin go hand and hand anyway.

49)   **DE-EMPHASIZE THE IMPORTANCE OF APPEARANCE**. *The Bible (1 Samuel 16:7) says "The Lord does not look at the things man looks at. Man looks at the outward appearance but the Lord looks at the heart".*
Now, I need to clarify something here... when I say "de-emphasize appearance" I, in no way mean that you should teach your daughter that it's ok to be slovenly. IT IS NOT! I have always taught my daughters to never leave the house without a once over or even a twice over in the mirror...always to ensure no tags are hanging out, no wrinkled clothes are attached to our bodies, and no dry, brittle-looking skin is screaming out to the world "Hey, look at me!"   When I say "de-emphasize the importance of appearance" I mean that daughters should be taught that very expensive name brand labels are not important at all. But there's more to this...I'm reminded of a story where
this homeless man came into a restaurant, dirty, smelly and unshaven. The daughter of the restaurant owner, with her nose turned up, frowned as the man walked thru for his daily cup of coffee. The restaurant owner would allow the man to clean up

in the back where she would always have a fresh, clean pair of clothes for him to change into. The daughter asked her mom "why do you keep letting him come in here as dirty and smelly as he is?" The mom took her daughters' hand and said "always, always be kind to EVERYONE you meet, because you never know when you might be entertaining an Angel." I've said this before but it definitely bears repeating: it doesn't matter what someone wears on the outside, or even if they're not the best dressed or the cleanest, it's what's going on on their insides that truly matters most.

50)   **SHOW HER HOW TO DRESS LIKE A MILLION BUCKS WITH CLOTHES FROM THE SALE RACK.**
I used to be a really big spender until I realized how much money I was wasting. Money that could be set aside for my daughters' futures, I was spending on expensive blouses and shoes and of course, handbags. Then one day, I decided I wanted to be known as a SAVER and not a spender, and that's the day I became A FRUGAL MOM! Although this has taken some getting used to for my daughters who of course were spenders just like me (yep, I created those monsters), they seem to be coming around slowly but surely. I can now walk into a department store and have no qualms about heading straight for the sale racks, and by refusing to purchase anything unless it is on sale has kept me in line and in order! *I have taught my daughters that you don't have to spend a million bucks to look like you spent a million bucks*. Just take your time and find just the right pieces that are on sale at the right times for you. There are tons of discount outlets popping up all over the country and believe it or not, this is where the Ladies with the real money shop! They'll just never admit to it. So, we'll just let it be "our" little secret. Even Michelle Obama is still shopping in the world famous TARGET (pronounced Tar-jay). You Go, Girl (oops, I meant First Lady!)

HER STRENGTHS

51)   ALWAYS FOCUS ON HER STRENGTHS, INTELLIGENCE, AND PROBLEM-SOLVING ABILITY.   DON'T DWELL ON HER INADEQUACIES.

The Bible (Philippians 4:8) says, "And now, dear brothers and sisters, one final thing. Fix your thoughts on what is true, and honorable, and right, and pure, and lovely, and admirable. Think about things that are excellent and worthy of praise."
No one is perfect; although on some sarcastic level (which I don't like at all!) my two darling daughters accuse me of being JUST SO PERFECT! "YES, MOMMY, NOBODY'S PERFECT BUT YOU!" they taunt. (Is it just me or does anyone else think that I should stop referring to them as ANGEL DAUGHTERS right now?) Anyway, moving right along...our daughters will stumble, just as we stumble, therefore we should make mention of their inadequacies only to teach and not to berate or put down in any way. They are so much more than their inadequacies, which is why we should lend more focus to their strengths, their intelligence and their problem-solving abilities.   "See, Daughters of mine, I said it. I stumble, too! Not very often, but I do." (Just kidding, because I know they're both wanting to just roll their eyes at this...but of course, they won't because they know better).

52) **EMPHASIZE INTELLIGENCE, HARD WORK, INDEPENDENCE, SENSITIVITY AND PERSEVERANCE**.

I'm not that old, still in my early thirties actually (I know, wishful thinking on my part, right?), but if my memory serves me well, in 1966 the legendary James Brown recorded a song called "THIS IS A MAN'S MAN'S WORLD." The lyrics attribute all of the productive work that goes on in this world to the male gender, but allows that it would all amount to "nothing without a woman or a girl." Well, that was clearly in the '60s…and we are now clearly in 2013 and this Lady begs to differ. Although I totally disagree with the lyrics of that song and the thinking of those times, sadly, that is still the thinking of some today. This is why, we as *Good Mommys must emphasize intelligence, hard work and perseverance. We have to teach our daughters to THINK like a man, but ACT like a lady at all times. Teach them to persevere and keep pushing no matter what! We have to instill in them hard-core work ethics because no matter the times, they will always, always be fighting an uphill battle against that metaphoric "glass ceiling."* And in all that, lastly, we must teach our daughters that sensitivity is what makes us SO VERY DIFFERENT from our male counterparts and SO VERY, VERY SPECIAL!

53) **TEACH HER THAT IT'S OK TO BE ASSERTIVE**.

 Unbeknownst to me, I often hear that we (Ladies) were put here to be meek and mild, and we have also, on many occasions, been referred to as the "weaker" sex. I am horribly offended when I hear this. Teach your daughters that meek and mild should be reserved for farm animals, not for a species as STRONG AND REGAL AS US! *Teach them to always be assertive in their dealings with others, to be confident and self-assured in all that they do.* This trait will open many doors for them professionally and will take them very far in life.

54)   TEACH HER THAT SHE CAN DO ANYTHING A MAN CAN DO, AND MOST OF THE TIME DO IT BETTER.

"What is the glass ceiling?" Well, it is "the unseen, yet un-breachable barrier that keeps women from rising to the upper rungs of the corporate ladder, regardless of their qualifications or achievements." The glass ceiling metaphor has often been used to describe invisible barriers ("glass") through which women can see elite positions but cannot reach them ("ceiling").   These barriers prevent large numbers of women from obtaining and securing the most powerful, prestigious, and highest-grossing jobs in the workforce. Moreover, this barrier can make many women feel as if they are not worthy enough to have these high-ranking positions, but also feel as if their bosses do not take them seriously enough. _When we teach our daughters that they can do anything a man can do, and most of the time, do it even better, then there will be no more "glass ceiling." We need to teach, that it is not ok to go around down-playing our intelligence, either just to pacify a man's ego._ THIS WILL NEVER BE ACCEPTABLE! I can't think of one thing that they can do that we cannot, BUT, I do know this…. both sexes have the right "to bear arms", but only WE can bear children!

55)   TEACH HER SHE'S SMART.

I know you're wondering "How do you teach someone that they're smart?" Well, you tell them that they are, continually and consistently! When they solve problems on their own, praise their intelligence! When they figure out that calculus equation without your help, throw a party!   Studies have shown that _when you constantly drill something into someone's head, they start to believe it_. Continually call someone "stupid" and notice how they eventually begin to act…well, the same goes for continually drilling home that someone is smart. So why not send a quick text message to your beautiful daughter right now and just say "Hello there, Genius!"

56)   **TEACH HER THAT IT IS OK TO BE SMART AND NOT THE SMARTEST**.

Sometimes when we know just how smart our daughters are, we tend to unknowingly put this extra pressure on them. We do this by allowing them to overhear us say things like "Oh yes, Claire is the smartest person in her class!" Now there are typically about 25 kids in a classroom, and your daughter is the smartest??? Well, even if she is, now's the time to teach her that it is OK to be smart and not the smartest in the room all the time. No matter how much you go around boasting about that 4.0 GPA she has.

INDEPENDENCE

57)   REALIZE AND ACCEPT THAT WHAT YOU ENJOYED WHEN YOU WERE A LITTLE GIRL JUST MAY NOT BE HER CUP OF TEA.

When I was a little girl, I loved to read, just as I do today. I simply adore books! I love how they feel, I love to hold them, hug them, sniff them…I think they are total awesome-sauce! I was a fan of Nancy Drew growing up. Anybody else? I read the entire series, even acted out a few of the stories with my siblings (against their wills, of course).   Anyway, my most favorite book of all time was and still is, *LITTLE WOMEN* by *Louisa May Alcott*.   When I became a mom to my first daughter, I couldn't wait to go out and buy her very own copy of this book.   It didn't move her at all. Not one IOTA!   Same thing happened with my second daughter, (another one bites the dust).   I was so heart-broken that the both of them could not get into that which I had loved SOOOOO very much. I then realized that just because they weren't into the books from my childhood that was OK. I learned to accept that just as long as they were reading good, clean material… that was really all that mattered. This also gave me the sense that more and more, they were becoming their own individual, independently-thinking selves.   Our daughters may not want to read the books of our childhood, they probably won't even care for our music, but what they will want from you most importantly, is you, accepting that they love you even though they don't necessarily love what you love.

58)   **TEACH HER HOW TO CHANGE A TIRE, USE AN ELECTRIC DRILL AND MOW THE LAWN.**

I remember as a young adult, I didn't even know how to pump my own gas. I was never taught. I had a car, but then I had someone to always fill my tank. My daughters were TAUGHT how to be self-sufficient and very independent of anyone else. Daughters should never have to depend on some guy to do anything for them (unless it's their Dad...and that's OK). I remember the first time my daughter called from college and told me that she was having her car inspected. I was shocked but so impressed. She said to me "My dad told me how to do all this." I was so proud of him for being such a good Dad and knowing that he needed to teach these things, but I was even more proud of her for being receptive to learning, even after having grown up with a much pampered Mommy, who to this day, pretends to not know how to even take out the trash. But my daughters do (and that's all that matters!)

59)   **TEACH HER HOW TO DO CHORES AND TO PICK UP AFTER HERSELF**.

When kids are toddlers and making their own little messes of their playthings, begin teaching them then how to pick up one toy at a time and return it to its rightful place. And yes, **everything** has a rightful place. When she's a bit older, teach her to cook, do dishes and laundry, make beds, mop floors, clean toilets, etc. One day when you visit her in her college dorm, or her new home, you will be glad you took the time to give those lessons. Remember, CLEANLINESS IS THE NEXT BEST THING TO GODLINESS! (At least in my book it is...and this IS my book!)

INTEGRITY & CHARACTER

60)   TEACH YOUR DAUGHTERS ABOUT HAVING INTEGRITY AND GOOD MORALS.

Integrity is regarded as the honesty and truthfulness of one's consistency of actions. It can also be regarded as the opposite of hypocrisy. *Make talking to your daughters about different morals such as integrity and how they relate to the real world, a top priority. Help them to see that a person whom others trust and who does what he or she says they will do, earns the respect of others. Furthermore, teach them to admire those who keep their promises and always stay true to their word*.

61)   TEACH HER TO BE A LITTLE KINDER THAN NECESSARY.

I'm sure, even if you've never read one page from the Bible that you've heard the golden rule of kindness: **"Do unto others as you would have them do unto you."** Translated, it simply means: treat others the way you want to be treated. Little acts of kindness involve holding the door open for the next person coming through, letting the person behind you go first in line, taking time out of your busy day to volunteer at a homeless shelter, and offering to pay for food for that little boy who doesn't have enough to buy his lunch. I am always in awe of my Angel Daughters who every time they see someone on the street holding a sign they rush through *my* purse to look for money to hand out the window. (I had to stop them one day because obviously they didn't read this sign close enough. It read: "I'm not going to lie. I just want a beer." Money immediately returned to purse). I remember one Sunday, after having picked my little one up from church, she saw a dog that was so frail and thin, its ribcage was showing. It was pretty evident that she hadn't eaten in several days and to make matters worse, she was carrying puppies. My daughter, who was around 10 years old at the time, was moved to tears. She said "Awwww Mommy, she's hungry. We have to go get her some food." Not being close to home where there was a ton of dog food because we are total dog lovers, we drove to the market to get some food, water and bowls for this dog, my daughter praying all the while that the dog would still be in the same spot when we got back. Once we did, there she lay, too limp and hungry to move. My daughter jumped out, poured the food and water, soothed the dog with her words, said goodbye and got back into the car. It's little acts of kindness such as these, even when it is just compassion shown towards an animal, which separates a kind, warm heart from a hard, cold one. *Always teach your daughters to go above and beyond when extending courtesy and kindness*. Then she will always be able to proudly exclaim: "GOD knows my heart." And he truly will.

62)   **TEACH YOUR DAUGHTERS TO BE HONEST AT ALL TIMES**.

I started teaching my daughters about the importance of always being honest when they were still in my womb. These were daily conversations, between mother and unborn child that took place no matter where I was. If you show them how to be honest, they WILL be honest. I remember when I was in labor with my second daughter. I was in so much pain (Moms of the world, I know you all can relate to this) that my screams could be heard miles away from the hospital, I'm sure. My sister, who was there along with my oldest daughter, knew that my child was terrified to hear me in so much pain. So, my sister gathered my daughter and my 3 year old niece up and headed for the elevator so she could get them dinner and also get them out of earshot of my piercing screams. At the time, the hospital had a policy that if you were NOT a sibling of the baby that was on the way, then you could not be on the maternity floor. Once they were on the elevator, my sister said to my daughter and niece, "If anyone asks, you two are sisters." I loved it when my sister came back and shared this story with me. She said that my <beautifully sweet> daughter looked up at her with her big, blue eyes and said... "Auntie Laura, do I have to say that?" To which my sister replied... "No, darling, you don't have to." I told her "Oh no, you know we don't teach her to lie under any circumstance." My sister said she could see that my daughter would have been so compromised had she had to tell this un-truth. I have never once asked my daughters to answer my phone to tell someone that I wasn't available, when clearly I was. I just don't let them answer my phone at all, and that's why there is this wonderful thing called voice mail. I also have never once asked my daughters to answer the doorbell at my home then tell someone that I wasn't there, when I clearly was. My daughters simply don't answer my door, unless instructed to do so. _When you show them that you are honest, they in turn will want to be honest just like you. Always remember though that this works in reverse also. If you show them that you are dis-honest, don't be shocked when you get a phone call from the mall saying that your little darling was caught shoplifting._ Never forget, they do what we SHOW THEM, and not so much what we TELL THEM.

63)   **TEACH THEM TO ALWAYS BE HUMBLE**.
The Bible (James 4:6) says "God is opposed to the proud, but gives grace to the humble." Most people don't even know what it means to be humble, yet you hear them claiming it upon themselves quite often. *The Bible (Philippians 2:3-11) says "Do nothing from selfishness or empty conceit, but with humility of mind let each of you regard one another as more important than himself; do not merely look out for your own personal interests, but also for the interests of others."* Often times,

humbleness in action involves putting others first. An humble person is someone who does not boast or try to impress themselves on others. They are generally quiet, meek and typically not self-serving. This is a good set of attributes to have, *so impress upon your daughter the significance of being a truly humble person.*

64) **TEACH HER THAT REPUTATIONS ARE FRAGILE AND THEY FOLLOW YOU AROUND**.
The Bible (1 Corinthians 4:3) says "I care very little if I am judged by you or by any human court." This is very important. In the hallway of my daughters' old dorm, there was a sign that hung in front of the elevator that read: **"Reputation is what other people know about you; Honor is what you know about yourself."** I've always taught my daughters to not care what other people had to say about them or better yet, to care even less what other people thought about them. Sometimes, we put too much attention into what's going on in the mind of others. This can really be the cause of many sleepless nights. But, we must teach our daughters that there are some areas where what people think and how you are perceived does matter:

 1) Your daughter should always value the opinion of her parents, mentors and other adults who truly have her best interest at heart; 2) daughters should always care about how they are perceived by prospective and very selective colleges and employers; and 3) anytime that it is beneficial to her success and the people who have a direct influence on it. The thoughts and opinions of her peers should matter very little to her, as sometimes these are born out of envy and jealousy. *We should say to our daughters "**YOU** are the only person who can define your reputation. **YOU** are the only person who can set the tone for it. Therefore, **YOU** should take great care in ensuring that it is always impeccable and above any kind of reproach."*

57

The Good Mommy on…

JEALOUSY

65)   TEACH HER HOW TO RESPOND TO INSULTS WITH CLASS.

Simply by saying "THANK YOU!" with a really big smile on her face and walking away. **The Bible (Proverbs 12:16) says "The vexation of a fool is known at once, but the prudent ignores an insult**." I'm sure you've heard the old adage "kill them with kindness." This is the perfect way to do it. **The Bible (James 1:19-20) also says "Let every person be quick to hear, slow to speak, and slow to anger."** There is no need to respond to insults in any form or fashion, if she so chooses. That'll really throw the person who is slinging the insult right off balance and soon they will learn that your daughter is not fazed at all by their little "digs." The perpetrator will soon give up and move on to insulting someone else. Hopefully, that person's mom will have read this guide, too and taught this very same lesson.

66)   TEACH THEM HOW TO IGNORE AND DEAL WITH JEALOUS PEOPLE.

I remember when my oldest was four years old and one day we were watching a news segment about a 15 year old girl in New York who had just been picked up by a modeling agency. The young girl was so excited, that she went to school the next day and shared the news with those she thought were her friends. A mob of kids, boys and girls alike, brutally attacked this young girl, all because she was pretty and they thought she was bragging. It was pure JEALOUSY. My Aunt, who was on the phone discussing this segment with me at the time said "Oh, they are really going to hate your baby because 1) she's so pretty, 2) she's got gorgeous hair, and 3) she has a beautiful voice." Although I was blown away by what she said, I knew that she was right. As a young girl in third grade, I began to experience firsthand the ugliness of the green-eyed monster. I was an avid reader and great speaker, even at that young age, and was always called upon to do extra things because of my voice. Therefore, I was very familiar with jealousy. What I learned though, was to ignore it and use it as a propellant for me to excel and soar even higher. There is a phrase the kids use today and it goes "Let your haters be your motivators!" and way back then, that's exactly what I did and I have instilled that in my daughters. *Teach your daughters that sometimes there will be those who will be envious of them for no reason at all. Tell them to smile at these "green-eyed" monsters, and just keep soaring higher.*

67) TEACH THEM TO NOT BE JEALOUS OF OTHERS.

The Bible (Exodus 20:17) says "thou shalt not covet thy neighbor's house; thou shalt not covet thy neighbor's wife, nor his manservant, nor his maidservant, nor his ox, nor his donkey, nor anything that is thy neighbors'." To covet is to have the strong desire for the possession of others' specific personal properties or relationships; going beyond simply admiring someone else's possessions to thinking "I'd like to have one of those myself." Coveting includes envy – resenting the fact that others have what you don't. There will be many times in life when others will have things your daughters do not have. *What we need to teach them at an early age, is that they should ALWAYS be happy for those who have things they don't, and know that when it is meant for them, they too shall have. In the meantime, smile and be very, very happy for your neighbor!*

68)   **DON'T BE JEALOUS OF HER OTHER MENTORS.   BE GRATEFUL**.

I find it a little humorous when Moms are jealous of the time that their daughters spend with other women who also love them. It could be a mentor, a grandmother (who the Mom didn't have a great relationship with herself), an aunt or the mom of one of your daughter's friends. Although some moms may not view this through the same lenses as I, I think this is a wonderful thing, especially since you have taught your daughter the importance of loving everyone. *Let's face it, we live in a world where everyone won't love your child, so when you find someone who truly does, don't be jealous of them, be grateful for them.*

LETTING GO

69) IF SHE WANTS TO CLIMB TREES, LET HER. IF SHE WANTS TO JOIN THE ARMY, LET HER DO THAT, TOO.

When she was in your tummy you dreamed of Barbie dolls, doll houses, and pretty lace dresses. But then she's out and all she wants to do is what she wants to do, and that includes climbing trees and playing football. Now, just because that's what she fancies now, doesn't mean that when she's all grown up she'll want to be a linebacker in the NFL, she's just feeling her way around. If she wants to do some of the things that are generally considered as "boy things," then let her. (Ever heard the term "Tomboy?") Maybe she'll grow out of this, maybe she won't. You will just have to wait and see. Oh, and if she comes to you with an enlistment letter from the military, whatever you do don't faint in front of her. Wait until she leaves the room and then have your little moment. After she's packed and waving goodbye to you at the airport, maybe headed off to foreign soil, cry your little Mommy tears then continue to love, support and pray for her until she returns home safely. In the midst of this "Mommy-storm," know that she's only doing what you have raised her to do…to grow up, to become independent (no matter how you want to always keep her with you), and to always follow her dreams.

70)   **ASSURE HER THAT SHE WILL ALWAYS HAVE A PLACE TO COME HOME TO**.

I know it's hard when our babies grow up, become their own people and become independent of us. Making grown up friends, pursuing careers, and even moving out on their own, pushes them further and further away from their baby cribs. But that in no way means that they are leaving YOU. They are only doing what we have taught and prepared them to do...to be able to take care of themselves. As our daughters grow and change, so does the relationship between mother and daughter. That relationship doesn't have to change for the worse, though. Even though their bedrooms are no longer upstairs or down the hall, that doesn't mean that sometimes they won't need to run home to snuggle with you, for a good Lifetime movie. It only means that it will take a little longer for them to get to you from across the city, maybe. *Let your babies know that they will always have a place to come home to, and that is wherever you are.*

LOVE

71)   TEACH THEM HOW TO BE LOVING.

When your daughter is showered with love and affection, what she will take with her every day is that, which she has been shown... plenty of love and affection. She only receives love; therefore she already has a very strong foundation of being a very loving person.

72)   PUT LITTLE LOVE NOTES IN HER LUNCH BOX AND SEND HER LOVE NOTES VIA EMAIL AND TEXT.

You cannot make your daughter feel any more special than when she's having a hard day at school (whether it's elementary or college), than for her to open up her lunch box, or her email or text messages to find a very loving note from you, JUST BECAUSE. I have seen the smiles on my daughters' faces when they have awakened from a long nights' slumber, stumbled blindly into their bathrooms, only to find post-it-love-notes on their mirrors. I have stood in the doorway many mornings witnessing this, and the feeling that I know they have being welcomed in to their days this way, is simply indescribable.

73)   TEACH HER SHE DOESN'T HAVE TO LOVE THE BEHAVIOR, BUT ALWAYS LOVE THE PERSON.

There will be times when our daughters are faced with the worst kind of people, and some of them just may come in the form of family members.   If the person behaves obnoxiously after a few drinks of alcohol, then they just might have a drinking problem, and that may be the only time they behave in this manner. We must teach our daughters to always, always love, no matter who, stranger and family member alike. They don't have to love the person's behavior, but they should always love the person.

74) TEACH HER THAT YOU CANNOT MAKE SOMEONE LOVE YOU, BUT YOU CAN BE SOMEONE WHO CAN BE LOVED.

There will be times when daughters fall into relationships that just aren't healthy for them. They will think that if they stick it out with someone who is abusive mentally, verbally and/or physically, that they will change the abuser's abusive ways and make him fall in love with them. This will never be true. *Teach your daughter this: We can't change others, we can only change ourselves. We also cannot make other people love us, but we can ensure that we are the perfect kind of person who is worthy of being loved.*

PEER PRESSURE

75)   STRESS THE UN-IMPORTANCE OF POPULARITY.
Sometimes girls are popular for all the wrong reasons. There are those who are popular because they are bullies and the entire school is afraid of them. And then there are some who are popular because they've dated the entire football team. Neither of these would be considered my kind of popular by any stretch of the imagination. We should strive to instill in our daughters that it is more important to be a good person with a good heart, great values, strong character and integrity, than it is to be the person who is LIKED the most. *Let's teach our daughters that it's more important to strive to have all of the positive attributes listed above than to try and win the next popularity contest. A strong character and integrity is withstanding, while popularity is definitely fleeting*.

76)   TEACH HER TO SURROUND HERSELF WITH POSITIVE, AMBITIOUS, LIKE-MINDED PEOPLE.
The Bible (1 Corinthians 15:33) says "Do not be deceived, bad company ruins good morals."   I've always been very much interested in who my daughters called "friends." I've also heard so many parents say "You can't choose their friends." Well, I beg to differ. I've drilled into my daughters' heads that you are the company you keep, so if you don't want to be associated with thugs, then don't hang around thugs. If you don't want to be known as a BULLY, then don't hang around bullies. Teach them to be the person that everyone knows is the girl who stays away from people who do, or get involved in "BAD" things.

Always involve yourself in your daughters' friendships. Get to know them and their families. Have them over for dinner or for a movie so you can get a feel of the kind of people they are. It is your job to steer your daughter in the right direction in this area of her life as well. If she's called a Ms.-Goody-Two-Shoes (what does that mean anyway?), then that's OK. It's much better than being called a BULLY or something much worse.

77)   PREPARE HER FOR PEER PRESSURE IN SCHOOL.

While in school, our daughters will be faced with some new challenging decisions. Some are not that serious like whether or not to play softball or basketball, but others involve serious moral questions, like "should I skip class?" or "should I change this bad grade on my report card so my parents won't be upset with me?" Making decisions at that age is hard on a child, but when other people their age get involved, sometimes influencing them to make the wrong choices, this is called **PEER PRESSURE**. When your daughters are being taught the difference between right and wrong at home, she may, more often than not, make the right choices when pressured. But, we should teach our daughters that it is OK to just walk away from the pressure. Remove herself from the group or person that's pressuring her. If there is too much pressure and she brings it to your attention, do address it with school officials. No one should be harassed to the point that it makes them feel uncomfortable. It's not always "cool" to be the only one saying **no**, but in my book, it makes you the "coolest kid" around!

78) **WHEN SHE IS A PRE-TEEN, SHE WILL START NOTICING WHAT PEOPLE HAVE. TEACH HER TO PAY MORE ATTENTION TO WHAT PEOPLE ARE**.

I find it truly disheartening that girls as young as 8 and 9 years of age recognize NAME-BRAND labels. They know more about a Christian Louboutin shoe (and if you don't know what this is, as I didn't, it's the shoe with the red soles) than they do about their 2nd and 3rd grade spelling words. This is something that should be immediately discouraged. *When our daughters come home saying "Little Sally wore a pair of Guess jeans to school today, I want a pair," this is the perfect time to explain to her that clothes and the labels on them do not make you a good person. They won't make you an honest person, nor will they make you a loving person. Let her know that you want her to care more about people's character and morals than what types of clothing they put on their bodies. Then let her know that when she's old enough to have a job and pay her own bills, that's when she can become close friends with Mr. Guess!*

ROLE MODELS

79)   PROVIDE HER WITH A GOOD ROLE MODEL…YOU!

Have you ever heard the phrase "be the change you wish to see in this world?" I simply love that! I admit to having moments when I feel like just being ugly. For no reason whatsoever! But then I think to myself: "Would you like it if you had to encounter someone who just felt like being ugly…for no reason?" The answer is always NO. If I want people to behave in a certain manner, then I first must behave in that manner. I must 'model' that manner, that behavior. That's exactly the way it is with our Daughters. If you want to raise a prim and proper lady, then you yourself must exhibit prim and proper ladylike-ness. If you don't want her to swear, then you should not swear in front of her. If you want her to be kind and respectful of others, then so should you be kind and respectful of others. If you don't want her to be loose and carefree with her body and men, then you should not parade a village of men in front of her. Our kids mimic what we do, not necessarily what we tell them to do. Both my daughters have excellent posture and both are also extremely manner-able. They didn't pick these habits up from the streets; I modeled the behavior for them. You be that which you want to see in your daughters. I can't stress this enough.

80)   **KEEP IN MIND THAT SHE'S ALWAYS WATCHING YOU. HOW YOU CARE FOR YOURSELF, HOW YOU CARE FOR THE FAMILY, HOW YOU HANDLE LIFE**.

Tip #79 says to "provide her with a good role model…" I have always wanted to be the most perfect example for my daughters. I wanted to be the lady that they wanted to grow into. Your daughter will see you sick, she'll see when you're blindsided by life's circumstances, she'll also know when you're hurting, angry and confused. But if you're optimistic through it all, it will teach her to display a positive attitude toward problems when they come her way. It's important that we as moms take very good care of ourselves, just as we always take very good care of our families. We must do this for the obvious reasons and also because our daughters are watching. How we handle the stresses of life, is probably how she will in turn handle her stresses when she's an adult. Remain poised, calm and always keep a cool head in the presence of your daughter. *Always leave home with nary a hair out of place, metaphorically and literally, and she in turn will ensure that she is perfectly poised when she steps onto the streets of LIFE following closely in your footsteps.*

81)   **BE POSITIVE IN YOUR SPEECH AND MANNER AROUND HER**.

If I can give you one bit of advice that you should definitely use, it would be this: *DO NOT have grown up conversations around, or in front of your daughters*! If you have an issue with your friend, your sibling or whomever, it is between you and that person only. The child should never be privy to this kind of negativity. Even if you're harboring negative feelings about someone, say for instance (you and your estranged mom), don't say things that might cause your daughters to feel negatively towards their grandmother. THIS IS WRONG if you do. You always want your daughters to feel love for everyone, even the people you don't necessarily get along with. Now, there are some exceptions to this rule. If there is a friend or family member whose interactions with your daughters might hurt or harm them in some way, then it's OK to sit your daughters down and explain to them why you feel the way you do about this person and why you don't want them to have any interactions with that person(s). Now that is definitely OK. Being positive in manner….. Hmmm let me think…OK, it simply means that you should for instance, refrain from all road rage when your daughter is in the car. Images of you flashing the middle finger at the driver in front of you, or screaming obscenities at the lady who cut in front of you in line is not something your daughter should ever have to witness or overhear.

RULES

82) **TEACH THEM THAT RULES ARE NOT MEANT TO BE BROKEN**.

I have never been the 3-strikes-you're-out kind of mom. In our home, there were immediate consequences when rules were broken, and not followed (punishable by me, not their Dad. He's always the good guy). Mind you, I can probably count on one hand how many times this has happened with my Daughters, but when it did, your first strike and you were out! When we don't set rules for our Daughters day one, then it's almost like they're raising themselves. When we teach that there are rules, this is also teaching them obedience. Breaking a rule is definitely being disobedient. In the real world, there are rules which MUST be followed, or there are dire consequences. Whether you get a speeding ticket and you forget to pay it, or you fail to file your taxes by April 15th, there are consequences if you fail to abide by these rules. I have always said that *"we should teach our children before the world steps in and does it for us."* I assure you, this is not what you want to happen. Set concrete rules today and enforce them with an iron fist.

*I must also point out that my take on rules only applied to that point and time when my daughters were of age and able to understand the consequences. This does not apply to little children who are still being taught the ways of the world and the laws according to YOU.

83) **SET CURFEWS AND STICK TO THEM**.
There will come a time when your daughters wish to begin dating. I recommend that you not start this too early, and anything earlier than age 16, is too early in my book. When there are dates, there must be curfews. When they head out the door to just hang out with friends, there must be curfews. We must clearly state what time our daughters need to be home and we should, as they MUST, adhere to that curfew. No matter what age, as long as your daughter is living under your roof, 12 midnight is an acceptable time to end a date or any other hang-out session. There are exceptions to this rule, such as when a party or event is not starting until 10pm or 11pm. At that time, extending curfew to between 1:00 and 2:00 am is acceptable, and only if they are of age. Anything later than these times, you leave yourself open for a whole new game-changing plan that you just might not be prepared for.

84) **ENFORCE THREE RULES EARLY ON: NO EYE-ROLLING, NO DOOR-SLAMMING AND NO BACK-TALK.**
Moms understand how little girls WANT to behave sometimes. We understand, because we used to be those little girls. *The three rules above should be implemented as soon as your little darling has started kindergarten and gets around other little girls who just might be allowed to behave in this awful manner*. Why start so early, you ask? Because remember, this generation is growing up a whole lot faster today. If you wait until she is almost taller than you, then it is too late to try and impose these rules. (Now you can try it, but I don't see that ending well for either of you). In my home, it was always understood that even a hint of breaking either of these rules could cost you your pretty little teeth. POP! ("Hello Mr. Dentist. My mom says to tell you that my teeth are on the floor."). I'm just saying'. (Oh, I'm just teasing...or, maybe I'm not!)

STARTING OVER

85) **TEACH THEM HOW TO BOUNCE BACK FROM SETBACKS**.

A setback is defined as an unanticipated change from better to worse. We all have curve balls thrown at us in life, and some of them hit us head on and extremely hard. We must teach our daughters that life won't be rosy all the time, but when life knocks us down, we need to get back up, dust ourselves off, and get back on track. This is real life.....and life is unpredictable. We wake up each morning not knowing what will come our way that day. But if we teach our daughters to always expect the unexpected, and to just have faith that it will all get better, she will fare well in this world.

86) **TEACH HER THAT YOU CANNOT START A LIFE OVER, BUT YOU CAN CHANGE THE WAY IT ENDS**.

Every mom wants her daughter to be successful. Every mom wants her daughter to have an easy road, and a very comfortable life, free of any kind of pain or heartache. Sometimes, even with the best rearing, our daughters stray and become people we don't even recognize. There are many influences in the world, some good and some bad and sometimes, our daughters are attracted and drawn to the bad. If this happens, all we can do is PRAY and ask that the Lord watch over our child and keep her in his care. When all your prayers have been sent up and received, the day will come when your child sees the error of her ways and she heads back to the fold, into the safety of your bosom and your arms. She may feel as if she has messed up royally and is too embarrassed to face the world as she once knew it. *It's at this time, that you should let her know that she cannot change what has happened in her past, but she can surely dictate her future from that point on.*

73

TEACHING MOMENTS

87) **START TEACHING AT A VERY EARLY AGE**.

Throughout this book you no doubt have heard me mention how I started teaching my daughters when they were both inside my womb. I truly did this. The first time I felt the both of them move inside me, I said "OK, you're awake now. It's time for our lessons." You might think this odd, but aside from telling them that they were smart, I would say things like "When you come out, and you learn to walk, you will not destroy Mommy's house or anything in it. You will not put your hands on the walls. You will put your toys away when you are finished playing with them," and so much more. I have a funny memory of my oldest while she was having a visit from her little friend. My daughter was 3 years old at the time and she was taking her friend up to her room. As the little girl trailed behind her, hands on the walls and not the railing, my little darling having turned around and noticed, said "No, you have to hold on to this. You can't touch the walls!" It was so cute, and I felt so proud. She **had** been listening and learning after all. These little darlings are so very intelligent. Their minds are like little sponges just waiting to soak up knowledge and they get that knowledge from us, what we teach them. So, let's start filling them up early. By the time they've reached puberty, it's all but too late. Start now and you will reap the rewards of your early teachings.

88)   **TEACH THEM THE WORD "NO" IMMEDIATELY.**

I remember the first time someone said NO to me and meant it...I was 33 years old.   My entire life I had been allowed to do what I wanted, to behave as I pleased, and to just have whatever my heart fancied. Mind you, the person who said NO to me then, was immediately expelled from my life because I felt as if I had been slapped in the face. That's how badly it hurt. Someone **should** have TAUGHT me NO a long time ago. But it was in that moment that I decided I would stop giving my daughters everything their hearts desired, and would start to sometimes just say NO.   Let me tell you, they went from expecting everything that they laid eyes on, to being very selective in their requests. The word NO worked wonders with my daughters, and if you start early enough, it will work a lot better and a whole lot sooner for yours. When teaching the NO lesson just remember, the sooner the better!

89)   **MAKE YOUR HOUSE THE HANG-OUT HOUSE, WHERE HER FRIENDS ARE ALWAYS WELCOME**.

You want to know what she's doing and who her friends are? Then make your house the hang-out house that everyone comes to and that all her friends *want* to come to. Make it very comfortable so they want to be at your place more than they want to be in their own homes. Why do this? Because you know that there is safety in your own home yet you have no idea what's going on in someone else's. Listen to the friends, should they open up and need to talk. Encourage always. I believe that every opportunity you have with a child, should be a learning opportunity for them and a teaching one for you. You will soon become "Mommy (insert last name here)" to more than just your own.

THE CHANGING TIDE

90)   BE HER MOTHER, NOT HER BEST FRIEND.

When my oldest was preparing to leave for college, 5 hours away, in a town foreign to me, to live with a roommate we'd never met, I felt compelled to meet with the family of this girl, especially since we were all from the same town. My daughter and her soon-to-be-roommate met for lunch a couple of times over that summer and on both occasions, the mom and I were in the same general vicinity, since we had dropped the girls off for lunch. On one occasion, as both I and the other mom were in the same mall, I suggested to the soon-to-be-roommate to ask her mom if she would like to meet me for a quick "hello." That time, as well as the next, she had a really odd excuse for not being able to meet. Fast forward to move-in day of college and who walks in the room, along with her girlfriend, toting her daughters' belongings, but ever-evasive Mom! We said our "hellos" and then I proceeded to explain how I had tried to connect with her over the summer to meet, since our daughters would be rooming together for the next year. She went into this spill about how she's so busy all the time, and how the reason her husband wasn't there moving things in now, was because he's so busy all the time, yada, yada, yada. Then, out of nowhere she blurts out, as she points in the direction of her daughter "We are totally BEST FRIENDS!" Since this statement came clearly out of the blue, I said, "Well, I am clearly the Mom here and my daughter is CLEARLY the child. My best friends range in ages from 35 years on up." I then went on to say that I had also expected to see her at orientation, but I had missed her there as well. She, in her little high school cheerleader bubbly kind of voice told me that she hadn't even
known about orientation until it was over, and that her

daughter had driven herself. I said "Well, that's probably because y'all are TOTALLY BEST FRIENDS! If you were serving in mommy capacity at the time, surely you would have known." She was so TOTALLY taken aback by my saying that. I shared that story to say this, our daughters don't need us to be their best friends, in fact, there's no way we CAN be their best friends until they are adults. I personally could never discuss the things that I discuss with my adult female friends who are my age, with my teenage daughter. It just wouldn't be appropriate and incredibly uncomfortable. That would be like sharing with a 4 year old what you and the dad had to do to conceive her. That being said, *leave the BFF stuff between Angel Daughters and their age-appropriate friends. You guys will have plenty of time, later in her life, to wear the Mommy/Daughter BFF badges together*.

91)   TELL HER THE TWO OF YOU MAY DISAGREE, BUT YOU WILL ALWAYS LOVE HER NO MATTER WHAT.

I remember when my eldest daughter was 11 years old; a mom came to me and asked "How do you handle arguments between the two of you? My daughter and I argue all the time" (her daughter was also 11). She really caught me off guard with this one, but as I recomposed, I responded "I don't argue with children. There are NO arguments in my house between my daughters and I. This would NEVER be allowed to happen in MY home." She looked confused and so I went on to explain to her that if your child feels compelled to disagree with you, especially at that age, she should keep those thoughts to herself. That's where a lot of parents get off track, allowing their daughters to behave as if they are their equals. They are not! And although I know that they have their own minds and thoughts, arguing with a parent is just disrespectful. I mean, I'm not going to argue with my mom and I'm an adult, a wife and a mother myself! Now there is a clear difference between an argument and a disagreement, in my book. So *when the two of you disagree (and hopefully by this time she is at least 16 years old), let her know that even though the two of you are not on the same page at the moment, you still and always will love her no matter what. Remind her though, that first and foremost, YOU are HER parent, not the other way around. When she's old enough, teach her that it's ok for the two of you to agree to disagree.*

92)   **RESPECT HER WISH FOR PRIVACY**.

Mommys just expect that we should know everything that's going on in our daughters' lives, and in their heads.   And although I personally feel that we should up to a certain point, sometimes they want and they need their privacy. They need to have their own space, their own room, all of this to house their own private thoughts. Thoughts that she just may not want to share at that moment with you.   But given the time and the respect, which our little "mini-mes" deserve, if and when she wants to share with you, she will. Until then, respect her wish for privacy.

93)   **JUST ACCEPT THAT ONE MOMENT SHE'LL BE CLINGY, AND THE NEXT SHE'LL BE PUSHING YOU AWAY**.

Remember when you were 9 years old, in third grade and all you wanted to do was be with your mom? Remember how you liked putting on her high heels and playing dress up in her clothes then putting on a fashion show just for her? Now fast forward 5 years... remember when all you could think was "I hate you mom?" and "My day at school was good, now may I please go to my room?"   Remember your mom knocking on your closed door and all she could hear was "I'm fine, I just want to be alone!" Now fast forward once again 10 years, and sure as Santa lives at the North Pole, mom can't get rid of you again! *So, when your daughter begins to exhibit all the behaviors listed above, all you need to do is sit back, think back, and wait it out. You won't be able to get rid of her, even at those times when you'd really like to*.

94) ACCEPT THAT BY THE TIME SHE'S IN MIDDLE SCHOOL, SHE DOESN'T WANT YOU TO KNOW EVERY THOUGHT IN HER HEAD.

Now this one was hard for me, simply because I had taught my daughters to tell me everything. And even today to some extent, they still do tell me everything, but the reluctance of telling me some things when I would ask is what bothered me. I had to accept and realize that they were growing into their own little people, who had their own little thoughts, that maybe they didn't want to share with Mommy all the time. We as moms, have to understand this and give them their space. This is a developmental time for them. This is about the time that they are hitting puberty and as their bodies are changing and developing, so are their minds. Don't worry, it will all come back around full circle and when you're old and gray in a rocker with a hearing aid, they'll tell you more than you ever wanted to know (although at that time, you may not be able to hear it).

THE INTERNET

95) TEACH HER ABOUT THE DANGERS OF THE WORLD WIDE WEB.

Kids today definitely know more than we do when it comes to the internet. So much so, that we go to them when we have questions about our computers and how to maneuver the "Net." This is not good at all. Too many kids are being caught up in the <www> and all its dangers. Pedophiles are sitting behind their keyboards encouraging our daughters to show them glimpses of their body parts. They're also enticing them with promises of gifts and a life free of parental control...(that's enough to make anyone give out their home address and phone number, right?). But seriously though, before we bring the computer into the house, sit your child down and explain to them that it isn't a toy. It's a very serious tool and its seriousness should always remain at the forefront of their brains. *Teach your daughter to NEVER give, or post her home address, phone number, name or any other identifying information anywhere online without your permission.* (My teenage daughter is not allowed to post any pictures of herself online). Also, *let her know if there is someone posting anything that makes her feel uncomfortable, that she is to immediately bring it to your attention. Always make the time to KNOW all the social networking sites your daughter is on (if she's allowed to be on any) and always, always know the passwords to those accounts. Just like a cell phone, let her know that these are ultimately your accounts, you're just being kind enough to let her use them. Another suggestion: keep the computer in the family room where it can be monitored by you at all times*.

Leaving it in your child's bedroom is highly discouraged. If your daughter has a laptop, which are in many homes these days, _ensure that you are the administrator on that computer as well, and do invoke your administrative privileges periodically to see what she's up to_. This little tip has left many moms in shock after having searched the net only to find nude pictures and much more of their little darlings floating around in cyberspace. Scandalous!

TRUSTING

96)   **MAKE SURE SHE KNOWS THAT SHE CAN TELL YOU ANY, AND EVERYTHING**.

My teenager and I have this little thing…when she was a little girl (and even now) she would come to me and ask "Mommy, can I tell you something?" and I would always respond lovingly "Yes honey, you can tell me ANYTHING." She loved to hear me respond to her in this manner, and I must admit, it felt good instilling in her that I would always be there for whatever she wanted or needed to share with me. Sometimes we fail our daughters in this area. We're so judgmental and harsh in our opinions of things, that we cause them to be afraid to come to us and share their deepest secrets and greatest fears. If you are guilty of this, you can still turn it around. Go to her and let her know that you are there to listen and only to listen if that's what she needs. Let her know that you're also there for encouragement, love, support and advice when she needs that, too. *Make sure she understands that there is nothing in the world she can't share with you, and no matter how bad she thinks something is, it will never change the love you have for her*.

97)   **REMAIN CALM, EVEN IN THE MIDST OF HER TELLING YOU SOMETHING YOU REALLY DON'T WANT TO HEAR.**

Remember opening the door wide for her to be able to come to you with anything? Well, here is your perfect opportunity. Sometimes our daughters will have things to share with us that will shock us. Sometimes, to our very core. But *we must remain calm in our words, our expressions and manner lest we make her feel as if she made a mistake by sharing with us. Listen first and when it is your time to speak, choose your words very carefully so as not to shut the door on her sharing with you the next time*. You can do this!

98) **TELL HER TO BE CAREFUL WHO SHE REVEALS HER PERSONAL LIFE TO**.

Here today, gone tomorrow. Those are the friendships of today. When I was growing up, we really were BEST FRIENDS FOR LIFE (BFFs). Today, it's hard to find true girlfriends and confidants. I heard someone say "We don't want anyone telling our personal business but then WE tell our personal business." It's true. We live in the internet/social networking age and for that reason alone, you should teach your daughter to be careful who she reveals her personal life to. If she isn't careful, someone she **thought** was a true friend could get upset with her and then everything she has ever shared with this person ends up on the World Wide Web. *Teach her to get to know people, I mean truly KNOW people before she allows them to wear HER BFF badge of honor. Continually remind her that if there is something you don't want anyone else to know, then KEEP IT TOTALLY TO YOURSELF*! (Or, hit rock bottom like me and tell your Grandmother!)

WHAT NOT TO DO

99)   DON'T ALLOW SLEEPOVERS UNLESS THEY ARE IN YOUR HOME.

My daughters have had a gazillion sleepovers AND I have been the hostess of all of them. When you allow your daughters to sleep over to friends' houses, you don't know what's going on there. You don't know how the other girls are behaving, if bullying is going on, if cuss words are coming out of the other girls mouths, if the hostess Mom is single with boyfriends in and out of the house all the time, if they're watching films that are too adult-like for your child…you just don't know, and that is entirely too much for you to have to worry about. *When you host the sleepovers, you set the tone for the behaviors at that sleepover. Even if you encounter a little "terror," you, being the hostess Mommy, are able to re-direct that behavior and teach the appropriate one*. I think sleep-overs are great bonding tools for girls and I would never deny my daughters this pleasure. But, they were always taught, that unless Mommy really KNEW the parents, I mean really, really, really knew, then all sleepovers would be at our house! (Oh, and in answer to your thoughts, I never really, really, really got to know any of the other parents that well).

100)   **NEVER DO DROP-OFFS**!

When my 20 something year old daughter was around 12, we took her, and a couple of her friends to see a movie. As the three of them all sat in the row in front of us, my husband leans over and whispers… "Look over to my left, but please don't say anything or you will bring attention to it and the kids will see." I did what he asked and what I saw made me furious! A young girl, who couldn't have been any older than 13 years of age, was sitting…no, she was STRADDLING a boy, skirt raised thigh-high and all, right inside the theater! Even in the dark, it was clearly obvious they were having sex. I had noticed the young two-some while we were waiting in line outside the box office. She, with a very, very short skirt on and he with his hands, palming her buttocks. I would stake my life on the fact that her Mom had made the grave mistake of "dropping her off."

The first time my eldest daughter was left in the mall unsupervised, she was 19, and she worked there. "Dropping off" at the mall, the movie theater, a theme park, etc. leads to a ton of trouble you never want to run into…an unplanned (teenage) pregnancy ranking #1 on that list. _Monitor and supervise your daughters until you are absolutely sure they are mature enough to handle situations, as well as control their young emotions and hormones without you being there_. I and/or my husband have had many trips to the mall where we followed very closely behind our little darlings and their friends as they traipsed from store to store, pretending we weren't there. _Teach your daughters that even when they are old enough to be left unsupervised, they should remember their manners and to steer clear of any situations that are not appropriate._

Acknowledgements

I'd like to pay homage to a few wonderful people who have supported and encouraged me throughout my life as well as the writing of this guide. The ladies here are all moms who have also raised (Almost) perfect daughters so they deserve my GOOD MOMMY AWARD!!! The guys that are listed are very awesome as well.

~~~~

J. Francis Rihel, whom I met when I was a mere 18 year old college student and who taught me so much about caring for others and mothering. I watched you care for your mother, all the while thinking that you were an Angel Daughter. I've also watched you raise your own daughter and do a magnificent job of it. You made it look too easy. Although I'm all grown up now, you're still teaching me with your resilience for loving and living, even in the midst of incredible challenges. You are one of the most warm-hearted and caring people that I have ever met and I am blessed beyond measure to call you my friend. I love you dearly.

B. Beverly, you have successfully raised 5 daughters. WOW! Now, that must have been hard. You were there even before I was born. You have encouraged and taken care of me, wiped my tears, held my hand and listened to all my fears. You have praised my parenting and there is no other compliment that has ever meant more to me. Thank you for all the times you let me read to you bits and pieces of **"THE GOOD MOMMIES GUIDE…"** and for sharing your honest thoughts. I love you and would be lost if you weren't here in my life nor would I be the mom that I am had it not been for you always making me feel like an Angel to you. Thanks for being my "rock bottom."

Kathryn Paige, my beauty queen "other mother." You have taught me what it means to grow older gracefully and I have watched you also be the mother who loved your children a little too much, too (if that's at all possible). You inspire me for being a GREAT daughter as well, and although I was never the kind of daughter you are, my wish is that my daughters will one day love me in my old age as you love your Mother. I wish I could give personal accolades to your grandmother because she raised you and in my eyes you are (almost) perfect, too!

Faith Waller, you are the greatest mom! The way your Angel Daughters love and treat you is a direct reflection of how you love and treat them. In many photos that we have taken together, you are looking at me with such admiration yet it is I who stand in awe and complete admiration of you. I often tell people that in your eyes, I can do no wrong, and that's why I wish everyone could borrow your eyes just for a day. Thanks for the phone calls to ensure that I was still "writing" this great work of art as you called it. Thank you for always being in my corner and for sending the naysayers running when they had nothing nice to say. You inspire me and one day, when I grow up, I want to be just like you!

Jean B ., although I have never met your daughters I do know that they have to be true gems because you raised them, and that's what you are to me. I love the way you continue to challenge me in my faith, as if you know that one day I WILL GET IT. I know that you want only the best for me and my soul, but know that I'm working on it and although I may not get there or be as strong as you are when I do, in due time I will be there. Thanks for helping me through my scriptures as only you could have done for me. Although you won't say it, I know you're very pleased that I included them in the book. Thanks for all your advice through the years in the rearing of my own daughters. Maybe one day you will know just how you kept me thinking and how you kept me continually wanting to know more about "the word," which always led me to asking the "hard" questions.

Evelyn Braxton, you and I have never met (at least not yet), but I TRULY AM AMAZED at how you parent your Adult daughters. I love how you refuse to accept any animosity between them and how you have raised them to love each other the way they clearly, obviously do. I speak of you often to my Grandmother who has never had the chance to watch the show, and she laughs every time I give her one of your famous quips, you know the ones that you use most often on Tamar. I hope that if the day should ever come when I need to tell my daughters "DON'T MAKE ME S_ _ _ THE P_ _ _ OUT OF YOU" (the way you do it), that they still feel loved even in that statement, and laugh at me as though I've lost my mind, knowing that it's only me loving them. It is evident that you have raised daughters who STILL respect you in their adulthood as they did when they were little girls.   Even now, though I have an adult daughter, your parenting style gives me hope that we will continue to be alright as mother and daughter. You are also NOW one of my greatest inspirations and if I am blessed to one day reach the age that you are, I hope to be as graceful and beautiful inside and out as you clearly are. Thank you.

Ron Walker, my Social Networking Marketing Agent and pal. Thanks for allowing me to whine through this entire process. There were days when I wanted to throw my hands up in the air but you wouldn't allow it, and I'm forever grateful to you for that. I so appreciate all the late nights that you stayed up with me and my many questions. And thanks for always running off to find my answers. I appreciate the great job you're doing and let's get this baby on THAT LIST and move on to the next!

Charles H., now this book would not be published now if it had not been for all that you did. Thanks for taking the time to put things in their place and more importantly, thanks for TEACHING me and forcing tutorials on me. You are a true genius in my book. Hopefully, I won't need you as much on the next one but if I do, I know that you'll be right there walking me through it every step of the way.

SOURCES

Chua, Amy. Battle Hymn of the Tiger Mom. Penguin, 2012

The Bible

ABOUT THE AUTHOR

NONNIE Jules grew up loving books and everything about them. She has traveled the world, jumped out of planes and climbed many mountains all thanks to the wonderful world of literature. She lives with her husband and two daughters on a very quiet strip of land in Louisiana, where red dirt and pick-up trucks go hand and hand. She continues to write from many different genres and hopes to teach and touch minds and hearts alike with her very unique style of writing. She loves positive feedback on her writing and personally responds to each and every email. Nonnie can be reached at nonniewrites@yahoo.com , on Twitter @nonniejules, on FaceBook (Nonnie Jules) and do follow her blog, WATCH NONNIE WRITE! at http://nonniewrites.wordpress.com.

You can find the book trailer to "THE GOOD MOMMIES' GUIDE…" on YouTube.com or by going directly to http://youtu.be/zg15rptFN2g

What's Next?

Daydream's Daughter, Nightmare's Friend
(a novel)
Trailer: http://youtu.be/qbUK3XQ5-dA
Due for release: the end of September, 2013

The Good Mommies' Guide to Raising (Almost)
Perfect Daughters II
Due for release: 2014

For autographed copies, great fundraising opportunities and for more info on Nonnie's books, please visit

www.nonniesbookstore.com

Mommy Notes:

Mommy Notes:

Mommy Notes:

Made in the USA
San Bernardino, CA
21 December 2014